Elias A. Long

The Home Florist

A Treatise on the Cultivation, Management and Adaptability of flowering

and ornamental Plants

Elias A. Long

The Home Florist
*A Treatise on the Cultivation, Management and Adaptability of flowering and
ornamental Plants*

ISBN/EAN: 9783337106171

Printed in Europe, USA, Canada, Australia, Japan

Cover: Foto ©ninafisch / pixelio.de

More available books at **www.hansebooks.com**

THE

HOME FLORIST:

A TREATISE ON THE

CULTIVATION, MANAGEMENT AND ADAPTABILITY

OF

FLOWERING AND ORNAMENTAL PLANTS,

DESIGNED FOR THE USE OF

AMATEUR FLORISTS.

By ELIAS A. LONG.

ILLUSTRATED.

BUFFALO, N. Y.
LONG BROTHERS.
1874.

CONTENTS.

THE HOME FLORIST.

INTRODUCTION.

THE cultivation of plants for the sake of their beautiful or fragrant flowers, and for other pleasing attractions, has from the earliest ages received attention wherever civilization has made considerable progress. Floriculture, however, is an art which is strikingly susceptible to influences of climate, soil, heat, cold and other conditions, and notwithstanding its antiquity, uniform and universal progression has been impeded by reason of this fact. Any experience and knowledge derived from the attainment of a certain degree of perfection in the art, during one age or in one country, when applied to another, is practically useful only to the extent in which it finds a state of adaptability in the other. In our own country the cultivation of plants and flowers has only of late years received much attention, while from the first it has been realized that a course of floriculture distinct from any practiced in foreign countries, would be a necessity, and after years of practical schooling, we may claim to have adopted a system which in the fullest sense is American. It has been within the last dozen years, that a general manifestation of interest in floriculture, by the masses of people has been apparent, and from a perceptible awakening early in this time, there has been a continual and rapid increase, until the present time, which finds nearly everybody devoting more or less attention to their culture.

What is felt to be the greatest need of the day is, the more general dissemination of practical, useful knowledge, for acquainting people with the kinds of plants and flowers most suitable for the American cultivator, and also their culture, all adapted to the wants of inexperienced amateurs. It is with a realization of this need, that the author and publishers of the present little work, take pleasure in presenting it to the public, as a book of instructions, relative to the proper means of managing plants for the adornment of American homes. It is designed to aid all classes of cultivators, but especially those who aspire to the rearing of a higher and choicer order of plants and flowers than are common in perhaps the majority of homes where floriculture has been receiving attention, aiming to carry those who adopt its teachings, over obstacles which tend to cause failure and discouragement, and to promote an interest in every plant, bulb, seed or tuber whose culture is attempted.

A good indication of progression in American amateur floriculture is evinced in the fact that people of floricultural taste are learning to act upon the knowledge that more than seeds alone, or bulbs, or plants, are required for beautifying gardens and homes with flowers; that in the best kept gardens, are used judicious selections of some of each, with most gratifying results. No matter, scarcely, to how limited an extent the culture of plants and flowers is engaged in, it can be more advantageously done, and becomes more interesting, by including in the stock cultivated, perennial greenhouse and hardy plants, bulbs, and tubers, annual and biennial seed-grown plants—than by limiting the stock to varieties of any one class. Where the stock must be purchased from the florist and seedsmen, this rule will hold good, with most any amount to be invested, no matter how small. I have seen gardens where none but annuals and other seed-grown plants were employed, which were beautiful and pleasing during the entire summer season; and I always advise persons who expend but little for floral decorations to depend largely on these for their flowers. But where richness of color, exquisite fragrance, and strong contrasts in foliage, are sought, some plants that are propagated and sold from green-houses, and also bulbs, etc., are unapproachably effective. Planting even a very few Scarlet Geraniums, Lantanas, Gladiolus, Heliotropes, Hyacinths and other hardy bulbs, monthly Roses, and others, add to the grounds a brilliancy of color, and afford abundant daily bloom, from early in the spring, until October, and with many, even in November, which find no equal in seed-grown things. It is also next to impossible to nicely stock a hanging basket, vase or window box without the use of greenhouse plants.

New beginners at flower growing are apt, sometimes, to have over-ambitious ideas in regard to selecting stock for their first attempts; they invest largely in all kinds of stock found in the catalogues of their suppliers, only to regret the injudicious step when the time of planting and cultivation comes. I advise those making first selections to begin by selecting varieties that are easily grown, gain all the information possible relative to the treatment they require, not over-looking the important matters of soil, time of sowing, planting, etc., and then give them the very best attention. A dozen choice plants, besides the production from half a dozen pack-ets of flower seeds, well cared for will give more real enjoyment to the cultivator than a hun-dred plants and other stock left in a neglected condition to take care of themselves. The most careful new beginner is likely to meet with little difficulties and drawbacks, which, by unpropi-tious weather, or other causes, are to be expected will attend floricultural operations. In these the young florist who has a love for the work and its fruits should find no cause for being discouraged. The most skilled florist has always something to learn ; and no mistake will be made but you will be wiser for it, and the better prepared for future emergencies. Suc-cess, gained at the expense of slight failures and inconveniences, will be enjoyed the more for them afterwards. After each succeeding season's experience you will see the safety of striking out more boldly in purchases and plans, and each year will place you higher up that scale to perfection which every cultivator of flowers aspires to.   E. A. L.

Buffalo, N. Y., October, 1874.

DO PLANTS POISON THE AIR WE BREATHE.—There is a notion prevalent that the presence of growing plants in the sleeping or living room is detrimental to a healthy atmosphere by their giving out poisonous carbonic acid gas in the night time. The investigations of chem-ists demonstrate that growing plants do exhale an almost imperceptible quantity of carbonic acid gas, which, in very small proportions, is necessary in the air we breathe. They also show that the quantity exhaled at night is but the one-sixteenth part of what the same plants *absorb* from the atmosphere during the day, and convert into nearly its own weight of oxygen, thus render-ing a poisonous gas, that derives its origin from various sources, into one of the principal ele-ments of pure air.

If carbonic acid gas is emitted from plants in dangerous quantities, it certainly would exist largely in the night atmosphere of a close greenhouse heated to a tropical temperature, and crowded from floor to rafter with rank vegetation. Yet, in my experience, I have never known the slightest ill effects to be realized from night work in greenhouses, neither in cases that have frequently occurred with workmen making the warm greenhouses their sleeping quarters of a night, and even for an entire winter, which, to my satisfaction, affords practical proof that the notion is a fallacy ; and the fact that perhaps no healthier class of men can be found than green-house operators, who work constantly in an atmosphere where plants are growing, would prove, instead, that living plants exert a beneficial influence upon the air we breathe.

NOTES ON LANDSCAPE GARDENING ADAPTED TO COMMON PRACTICE.

As being somewhat distinct from laying out ornamental grounds, parks, etc., of large extent, the present article is devoted to that more limited branch of rural adornment, in which the majority of people outside of crowded districts in large cities are interested, namely : the beautifying and improving of grounds of moderate extent, which lay adjacent to dwellings—the planning of which usually devolves upon the owner or occupants of the place. That a marked degree of incongruity and dullness is observable in the surroundings of the majority of American homes, cannot be denied, but this arises far oftener from lack of sound and useful information, ignorance of correct principles, and through not fully realizing the importance of thoroughly executing work of this nature, than from want of appreciation of what is tasteful and elegant in ornamental gardening, in the minds of the people.

What is Desirable in a Place.—To be most delightful, a place of residence should be surrounded with ground of sufficient area to devote to ornamental purposes of lawn, flower beds, walks and drives, and for admitting the planting of shrubbery, trees, etc., in groups or singly. The area need not be very extensive to allow of this, and be rendered very attractive and pleasant, provided the various parts are arranged in good taste, and all operations which contribute to their improvement and after care are thoroughly performed. In all cases of improving grounds the house should be considered as the chief feature with which we have to deal, and the chief point of vision in a place. When the house is already standing, and the grounds have been improved in a measure, perhaps, it may be desirable to introduce some new improvements or to remove or alter any features which it is shown are objectionable; while with homes still in contemplation, we have the advantage of being able to arrange the various features at will, giving to each ample study and forethought, and finally deciding upon such a plan as combines the greatest number of excellencies.

Largeness of extent is desirable in ornamental grounds, but the fact that everything connected with constructing and maintaining them requires considerable labor and expense, should never be lost sight of. In every instance it would be better to decide upon a retraction of area, than to attempt work on a large scale with too small an outlay. Surroundings consisting of a fourth of an acre of land, improved in the most perfect manner, will be infinitely more satisfactory and enjoyable to the owner than a half or whole acre, with the same amount of labor and expense bestowed upon their improvement. There is such a thing, too, as augmenting the appearance of extent, in a place, be it large or small, and it would be well for all to study the subject who are interested in this matter. A garden—no matter what its size may be—will always look meagre in breadth without a good open lawn, and one broad glade of grass at least should, therefore, stretch from the best windows of the house to within a short distance of the boundary, at the farthest point, if the place be small, with as little interruption from walks, trees or other objects as possible. Harmony of parts and simplicity of arrangement also maintain the idea of size, for where everything is linked together to form a united whole, there will be none of that division of interest which tends to make a place appear still smaller. A place that is laid out in a formal manner—in the geometrical style—where all walks, flower beds and plantings are arranged with a degree of regularity, in which the various lines and parts bear a geometric relation to each other, will, unless very extensive, always look smaller than it really is, and very much less than one treated in a more irregular and natural way. Where the space will at all justify it, the walks, shrubs, flower beds, etc., should be so disposed of as to afford as many different views as possible. Walks, in which graceful and easy curves are introduced, are more pleasing than if made entirely straight, especially in small places, as straight walks or any straight lines require length to show them to advantage.

Trees and shrubs should be located mostly in groups at various points about the grounds— making the plantings heavier next the boundary fences—in preference to the style of planting in straight lines, parallel with the walks. The projections, made by curves in the walks and the points formed by angles, are suitable for accommodating groups, and these may extend back from the walk somewhat, but the inner points should be limited to such a distance as will keep the center of the grass plat open. It will be allowable, however, even in a small place, to plant here and there a small irregular group, or a single tree or shrub, which is notable for its fine form and appearance, while in large plans, with extended areas in lawn, large groups may be set with a view to breaking the distance and opening new scenes or parts in the grounds.

Flower beds are most effective if located in outward bends, formed by walks, or in chaste, well-balanced designs across the walk and opposite a bay or other window of the dwelling, or arranged, either as borders or else as numerous small beds, of round or other forms, on each side of walks, or at distant points across the lawn, to be viewed from the dwelling or street, and in other similar places. Sometimes an excellent effect is created by making them in the line of the walk, with the walk passing on each side, as shown in Fig. 14.

Where there is an opportunity of connecting a lawn with a closely fed meadow or pasture lot, which is almost on the same level, separating the two by means of a wire fence or a sunk fence, constructed in a depression, either natural or artificial, a place will be much enlarged in appearance. Trees may be planted in such a meadow, which will impart to it a park-like character.

It is frequently possible to keep some object outside the grounds in view from a principal window or garden seat, and where, from its attractiveness, it may seem desirable to do so, the planting of trees should be done to effect this. It may be a neighboring village, a distant mountain peak, or a steeple, or some edifice possessing an air of romance, and, perhaps, the plantings may be so arranged as to give it a beautiful setting between the trees, as it were. By Fig. 1 it will be seen how, if a desirable view is in the direction of *A*, the trees should be planted on each side of the line of vision, to keep the object in sight. Sometimes an object in some direction possesses an offensive appearance, making it desirable to shut it from sight. In the same figure we will suppose such is the case in the direction of *B*. It is plainly noticeable how trees can be thrown across the line of vision to entirely hide the object. For this latter purpose, evergreens are to be preferred, because of their being continually in foliage.

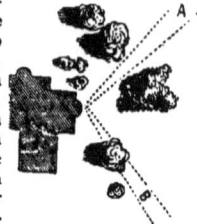

Fig. 1.

A few Things to be Avoided.—In the first place let me say, avoid attempting too much by applying the labor and expense necessary to put a place of certain size in order to one of twice or three times the size, and consequently doing the work only one-half or one-third as well.

Simplicity is a prime element in beauty, and nothing can be more objectionable, in small places especially, than intricacy of design, or the prevalence of an air of ostentation. Avoid crowding numerous flower beds or groups of shrubs or trees about the lawn, especially if it be a small one.

In deciding upon a plan for your place, avoid the two extremes of exposing it too much, or of rendering it too secluded by planting too many, especially of large growing trees. Errors are frequently committed in planting Hardy Evergreen and Deciduous trees, by not taking "one long look ahead." Many instances have come under my observation where Norway Spruce, Pines, or other trees, which, with age, grow to large size, have been planted while small close to walks, or perhaps the fence, house or other trees, in groups, without calculating for their future growth or spread. Such mistakes are not so evident to the planter while the trees are young, but after some years of growth, and after it is too late to remedy the matter, they encroach upon the walks or house or injure other trees, which it is now also noticeable where planted too close.

Planting ornamental trees is a work requiring forethought, and it is not altogether for the present immediate effect that it is done, but for time far distant as well, and one needs to have the full-grown form, size and appearance in his mind's eye at the time of planting, if he would avoid making blunders which never can be corrected.

Never locate walks and drives unless there is either a real or apparent need of them. They may lead to a flower bed in the lawn or to a seat or arbor, or be carried through the outskirts of the grounds, but there should always be a meaning connected with their existence— some objects of interest in close proximity to them, or to be seen from various points along their course. A writer of note has well said that "a walk leading nowhere and ending in nothing is never satisfactory." A practice which should never be allowed in walks and drives is for two bays or two projections on the same side to be seen at once. Use curves, as many as may be desired, but no serpent-like twistings. Avoid, however, making the curves too short; they should be fair and continuous, and reasonably direct, otherwise in a roadway a horse drawing a carriage would be likely to shave projections and avoid the indentations, and the track of the wheels would soon show the fault of the design.

In this country, where we are subject to severe dry spells almost every summer, terraces (earth thrown up above the common surface, and made uniformly level, usually,) should, as a rule, be avoided, unless means are at hand for watering the grass growing upon them whenever necessary. The same might be said of rockeries, unless they can be constructed in a shady situation, or where they can be readily sprinkled in dry weather.

The introduction of miscellaneous ornaments about gardens, such as statuary, groups of stones, artificial basins of water, or other objects of similar nature, should be undertaken with caution, for although there are places in which these may be desirable, yet it is easy to have more than are compatible with correct taste. A vase filled with vigorous plants seldom appears out of place.

Planning the Work.—The best time to avoid the bad effects which naturally arise from a poor arrangement of ornamental grounds, is before the work is commenced. How this may be done, is, by making an outline plan of the grounds to be improved, upon paper, locating existing objects, such as the dwelling, outhouses, trees that may be standing on the grounds, the highway, etc., in their correct position on the map, and then, with a pencil, do the planning throughout upon this, until a satisfactory plan has been arrived at, which can be transferred to the grounds in parts, as the work of improving goes on. It does not require much skill to draw the necessary map for this purpose, as the grounds or their outlines serve to guide the making of it, and with a pencil, rubber, and foot-rule (with the inch and the divisions of the inch marked upon it) you can get along well enough, as regards drawing instruments. First measure each boundary with a measuring tape—or a ten-foot pole will do (land surveyors would use a Gunter's chain, but the tape or pole will answer for ordinary use quite as well), representing each in its relative position on the paper, by a line reduced to a certain scale—say an inch, or any division of the inch, to represent ten feet on the ground ; then measure the distance the house and other objects are from the boundary line, and from each other, locating each correctly on the map, by measurement with the scale adopted for the boundary lines. Being these, and the boundary lines are objects, which will not be changed in the design, their outlines may be drawn with ink on the map, to prevent their being erased by subsequently using the rubber. The map is now ready for locating the various features to be introduced into the plan ; this should be done with a lead pencil, to allow of erasing and changing as often as may be necessary, until a plan is found which seems best suited to the place and to your wants. Everything should be drawn by the adopted scale of measurement, and located in its correct position, so that it can easily be transferred to the ground, by measuring, when operations are under way. Occasionally, as the work of planning progresses, each feature should be viewed from various directions, by holding the upper surface of the paper nearly in line with the eye ; this will give a better view of them, as they will appear on the grounds, than when seen by looking in a perpendicular line down upon the paper. The reason of this is obvious, when we consider that objects upon a landscape or garden are viewed, in this way the beholder standing upon the level of the grounds, and not above them.

It is well to make several maps, and draw a different plan upon each, thus securing the means of making comparisons, and choosing the one which combines the greatest number of good points. Fac-similes of the first map are easily produced for this purpose, by laying this one on top of half-a-dozen or less papers of the same size, and then thrusting the point of a thin pin-like instrument down through the papers at the corners of all angles, and the various points on the map. This will leave distinct marks on each paper, which will serve to guide drawing the lines for making each a fac-simile of the upper one. Too great care cannot be taken in making various plans and in finally deciding upon one, and any inconsideratenesss in these respects may be the source of regret afterwards. This is work for the leisure hours of winter, and it should be engaged in early enough, so that each and all distinct features that suggest themselves, may be deliberately pondered over and studied in their relation to the whole design, for, bear in mind, when a plan is once fully decided upon, and the work of completion executed, it is done for a long time distant in the future, and will stand as a monument, pointing either to the wise and deliberate or to the reckless action of the projector.

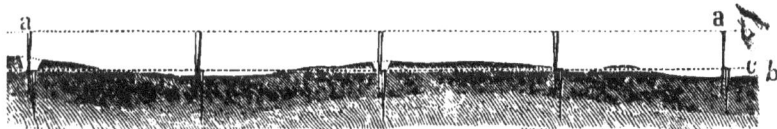

Fig. 2. Arranging Stakes to facilitate Grading.

Grading and Leveling.—After the plan has been completed, the work of grading the surface, which is generally more or less uneven, is first in order if it has not been done previously. Grading is one of the distinguishing features of a complete garden, and if nice and evenly done, does more to give to grounds, otherwise well improved, a finished appearance than any other one operation. The lawn if properly made will then present the appearance of a carpet of velvety green, and flower beds, shrubs and trees will stand in delightful relief above the surface. The propriety of preserving natural undulations, or attempting artificial variety of surface in moderate sized or small grounds, is always questionable ; although in large grounds planted in irregular style these, if softly and appropriately finished off, may be made to improve the general appearance of the grounds. The work of grading is commenced by passing over the grounds and leveling, being guided only by the eye ; all elevations should be plowed up, and the ground from them should be hauled or scraped into the depressions which may exist. It should, however, be observed that at least six inches of good soil overlay the whole in all places, and where any considerable hills are removed, sufficient subsoil is also to be removed to be replaced with top soil to this depth. Wherever walks and drives are to come, the ground may now be excavated to a proper depth for filling in with the road material, and be used in low places. When this rough grading is completed, drains should be laid wherever necessary, after which the work should be planned for finishing the grading to a nicety, and to do this it will be necessary to set guide stakes in rows across the grounds, driven down so that the heads be in line, and exactly marking where the new surface is to come. To accomplish driving the guide stakes so that the heads will thus be in line I shall presently explain. If a heavy rain can be had on the grounds before the work at this stage is advanced, it will be all the better, otherwise it will become necessary, with the finishing work, to leave the ground sufficiently elevated wherever filling in of low places was done, to allow for what the loose earth will settle. In Fig. 3 we will suppose the ground on each side of the dwelling

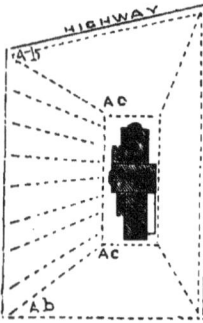

Fig. 3.

slants away towards the boundaries. The first step to take towards setting the stakes for guiding the work of final grading is to pass along the boundary and drive a stake at each corner of the lot to a depth so that the head is at the desired height for the to be grade in each place. Then drive four corresponding stakes also to a depth at which the head will indicate the desired surface when completed, around the dwelling, setting each far enough from the corner to enable sighting from it to the next one to it on all sides of the dwelling. After this, stakes are to be set in rows across each section or slant of the grounds to guide the leveling; but, as this can only be done over one part at a time, we will illustrate how to proceed by directing the reader through each step of setting the stakes on the wide plot of ground on the left of the house in Fig. 3. Let us suppose that the line *b* in Fig. 2 represents the surface between the corner stakes driven at *A b* and *A c* in the upper part of Fig. 3, and that the stakes shown at each end of this sectional cut, with their heads to line *C*, are these two corner stakes (*A b*, *A c*, Fig. 3). Now drive a stake at the side of each of these stakes, but with the heads, we will say exactly, 18 inches above them. These stakes are for the purpose of sighting over to place three or five or more stakes between the two corner ones. One person should sight while another drives the stakes; the former observing and directing the depth they are to be driven. This sighting is illustrated in Fig. 2. After these intermediate stakes are set, another stake should be driven at the side of each, with the top 18 inches lower than top of the sighting stake, which it is obvious will. bring the heads of them in line with the corner stakes just driven, as is shown by dotted line *C* in Fig. 2, which is the line of the desired grade. We next proceed with the sighting and staking operation along the boundary, from the upper corner stake *A b* to the lower corner stake *A b*, and also from *A c* to *A c*, driving the same number of stakes on each, although line *A b A b* is much longer than the other. The distance they are to be apart on each line may be arrived at by guess, as it is not material that they be exactly the same distance apart. A good way is to set one at what would be taken as half way between the corner stakes, and then dividing the distance to the corner on each side in the same way, and so on until enough have been placed, being certain, however, that the same number are on each line. After this is done, crosslines of sighting and guide stakes are to be run from each stake in line *A b A b* to the corresponding stake in line *A c A c*, in the manner described in my reference to Fig. 2, commencing at one end of the plot. The other quarter sections around the house are each in turn to be laid out in the manner I have described, after which the work of leveling may finally be completed. With these stakes at ten, fifteen or twenty feet apart each way, it is easy to grade the earth evenly between them. With the completion of grading and the removal of the stakes, we are brought to making walks and drives, and sowing the lawn, each of which are considered in a separate article.

The Lawn and Tree Planting.—A good lawn, clean and well kept, one which presents a lively green appearance, from early in the spring until cold weather, is a sight worth witnessing, and one well worth expending some labor and money upon to obtain. After the ground is shaped to the desired grade, as described above, then the whole should be thoroughly plowed, a sub-soil following in the wake of the common plow until it is thoroughly pulverized. The soil from the first furrow made in plowing will be thrown above the common level, and after the piece is overturned this should be drawn or wheeled into the open furrow left by the plow in finishing, that all may become even again. A heavy harrow should then be applied until the surface is thoroughly fined down. It may now be noticed by the careful eye that slight undulations still exist here and there about the grounds; these can be leveled with a shovel or hoe. All stones, roots, etc., should also be removed so that a smooth surface may be obtained; these will be found useful for filling, in making walks and drives. To facilitate the work of tree planting, which next should receive attention, small stakes should be set at the points marked on the plan; the planting should be done carefully and without unnecessarily digging or disturbing the graded surface. After this the harrow or, better yet, the rake may again pass over the surface, with afterwards the roller, and the lawn is ready to be sown. For small plats, of course, digging, trenching, and raking must be done, instead of plowing, sub-soiling and harrowing. Do not fall into the common error of using seed sparingly. Four bushels to the acre is the proper quantity. I do not consider it very important what kind is sown. The Red Top or Blue Grass are about the best, or the "mixtures" of desirable kinds. It is well to add a pound or two of Sweet Vernal grass to the acre, for the delightful fragrance it emits; also a quantity of White Clover, say one or two pounds to the acre. These are usually included in the mixtures prepared by seedsmen.

When the seed is sown, a light harrow or rake should be applied, and after that a thorough rolling given, so that the surface become as smooth as possible. The seed may be sown any time during the months of April and May, and will form a good lawn by August, if the preparation has been good. If sown in the hot months of June or July, a sprinkling of oats should be sown at the same time, so that the shade given by the oats will protect the young grass from the sun. Frequent mowing of the grass—and, let me add, weeds, also, for the first few months at least—should be attended to. The weed seed lying dormant in the ground at

sowing time, will spring up thick and rank with the grass, but will finally succumb to the frequent use of the lawn mower or scythe, while the grass will improve in strength and appearance with each cutting. Mowing every week or two will not be too often. The grass should be raked off after each mowing with a fine-toothed rake. Lawns are frequently sown during the early fall months with excellent results.

Sometimes after a good sod has formed on the lawn, it is desirable to remove a tree or shrub from one part of the grounds to another, or to plant a new one. In Fig. 4 we illustrate how this can be accomplished, without mutilating or otherwise injuring the sod, by making four cuts, two or three feet in length, away from the tree, and rolling the sod back while taking up or planting, and again unfolding it into its original position after the soil has been properly leveled. With a little care this operation may be so nicely performed as scarcely to leave any visible marks afterwards.

Fig. 4.

Sodding.—The edges of grass-sown lawns, bordering on walks, drives, flower beds, etc., should, for protection, be sodded one or two feet wide, with turf obtained from an even grassy spot in the meadow, where no weeds are growing, and cut into square blocks, or into lengths of five or six feet and one foot wide, which can be conveniently rolled up for handling; they may be cut two inches thick and should be laid closely and compactly together, beating down smooth with the back of the spade, so that there will be no crevices between the cut portions or beneath them. This work is best done early in the spring or late in autumn.

Walks and Drives.—Good dry roads or walks are a great comfort about the home, and when well made and finished they impart decided character and finish to grounds. The ordinary method of securing the curves which has been decided upon, is by measurement or by setting small stakes on the line of the road, and moving them until the curve seems graceful

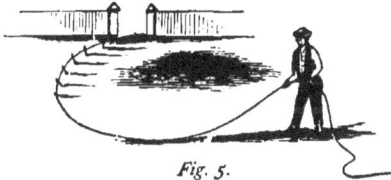

and pleasant to the eye. We find a very good plan in J. Weidemann's excellent work on Landscape Gardening, published by the Orange Judd Co., for accomplishing this. In the engraving, it will be readily seen how, by means of a stout cord and stakes, the curve is secured. After the desired course and width of walks and drives are decided upon, the work of making may commence. Excavate from one

Fig. 5.

to two feet, fill in with large stones, upon these put smaller ones, diminishing the size as the surface is reached, and finish off with coarse gravel, and then with a coat of finer, roll well, and there will be a road that will need little mending and fit to travel in all weather.

Designs for Flower Beds on the Lawn.—With a ten-foot pole, two stakes eighteen inches long and a cord to connect them, and several dozen small stakes for defining outlines, the following designs may easily be made. In Fig. 6 ascertain the points of the star by setting five stakes at equal distance from each other on the circle; lay the ten-foot pole from each stake to the second one from it both ways, and mark with a pointed stick. For the Moon make one large circle for the circumference, and another smaller with the center a little moved to give the inside shape. To make an Oval, first lay out an oblong square of the desired size, placing stakes at the corners. Then set five, seven or any like number of stakes, on each side, as is shown in Fig. 7. Now lay the pole against the middle, long side stake, and the first stake from the corner on the short side, and draw a mark; then move it to the stake next the middle on the long side and stake number two on the short side, and draw another mark, proceed in this manner around the entire square, and a well-proportioned oval will finally result. Triangular and other forms are readily made with the pole, stakes and line.

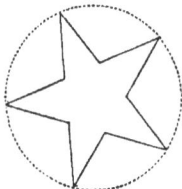

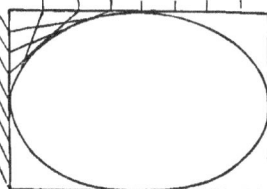

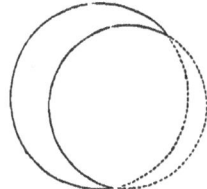

Fig. 6.   *Fig. 7.*   *Fig. 8.*

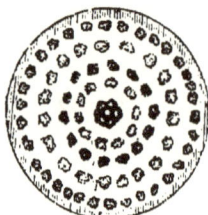

FIG. 9.   FIG. 10.   FIG. 11.

Figs. 9 and 10, Designs of Compound Flower Beds.   *Fig. 11, a Circular Ribbon Bed.*

OPEN AIR FLORICULTURE.

Planting in Masses of Color.—This style of adornment with plants and flowers is one of the most effective that can be adopted, when applied to ornamenting the grounds about the home, and it possesses the merit of being exceedingly simple. It consists of planting beds which are cut in the lawn, or otherwise located, with a single kind of plant, or with various kinds, arranged in groups,—the object being to plant so thickly that the ground will become entirely concealed, thus creating the effect of one or more, as the case may be, individual and distinct masses of bloom or color. Or the beds may be of compound form, consisting of separate parts, each planted with a distinct color. Sometimes an edging of a beautiful plant may be uniformly set around these masses, with good advantage. Only certain plants are desirable for planting in masses, being such kinds as are of free blooming habit, or which have attractive foliage of distinct form or color. Several designs of beds suitable for this purpose are represented herewith, and the reader is referred to the article on "Laying out Flower Beds in the Lawn," for others. It should not be inferred that beds planted in this style need be either large or costly to be effective. Beds three, or even only two, feet across, if cut in the green lawn, and planted with such valuable plants for this purpose, as Gen. Grant Geraniums, Coleus Vershaffeltii, or others, say five well-established plants for the smaller, and eight for the larger sized bed, will become amazingly attractive, and appear complete in any grounds. Amateurs trying one or more beds in massing could scarcely fail to be pleased with the result. Fig. 12 is a perspective representation of a round bed planted in three different colors, as shown by the dark and light colors. The centre is occupied by a distinct color and variety, somewhat taller than the others. Fig. 9 represents a compound bed of circular outline. The centre bed may be divided into four equal parts, each planted with a distinct color of Phlox Drummondii, or only two colors, as white and brilliant scarlet, each color occupying two opposite quarters. The small outside beds might be planted with mixed Pansies, and the large ones respectively with crimson and rose-colored Portulaca. Fig. 10 is a very easily planned compound bed, more elaborate than the last one described, but, like it, is well adapted for any grounds. The former may be twelve feet in diameter, from outside to outside, and the latter twenty-four to thirty feet across, between extreme points. A star, the body of which is planted with Achryanthes Verschaffeltii, and the points with Alternanthera Versicolor, a plant of the same color, forms a very attractive ornament. We have planted round beds with the dark and other colored Cannas, placing a row of White Centaureas around the edge with the most pleasing results. There is in fact no limit to the forms and varied arrangement of plants, which may be adopted with pleasing effects in this style of planting. To render the present article on this subject more complete, I give a list of the plants best suited to this purpose. The reader is referred to the description of each kind, which will be found in other parts of the work.

Ageratum in variety.	*Centaurea Candida,* and *Gymnocarpa.*	*Leptosiphon,* various colors.
Abutilon Thompsonii.		*Lobelia.*
Achryanthes, various colors.	*Coleus Verschaffeltii* and others.	*Pansies,* various colors.
Alyssum and *Thyme,variegated*	*Dwarf Convolvulus.*	*Petunias,* various colors.
Alternantheras, various colors.	*Geraniums, Gen. Grant* and others.	*Phlox Drummondii,* var. colors.
Artemesia Stellaris.		*Portulaca,* various colors.
Candytuft, various colors.	*Golden Feather Feverfew.*	*Stocks,* various colors.
Cannas, various colors.	*Heliotrope.*	*Verbenas,* various colors.

Ribbon Gardening.—This method of ornamental planting consists in placing plants with distinct contrasting colored flowers or with showy foliage, in lines either circular on round or oval beds, or straight on borders or square beds ; this produces an effect somewhat resembling a ribbon when viewed from a distance. To give a correct idea of this matter, I illustrate in Fig. 11 the placing of the plants in position in a circular bed; it will be seen that the work of planting may be guided by striking circles, with a line attached to a stake in the center. I have found in practice that in planting circular or oval ribbon beds it is best to plant the largest or outside circle first, finishing in the center. Fig. 13 represents a long ribbon bed planted with five lines of plants of various colors. One of the finest specimens of ribbon planting which I have seen, was a large oval bed 12 by 18 feet in diameter, with the first row

Fig. 12. Planting in masses of color.   *Fig. 13. Long Ribbon Bed.*

next the edge planted with Variegated Sweet Alyssum, eight inches apart, the second from the edge with Alternantheras ten inches apart ; third, Centaurea Candida, fourteen inches apart ; fourth, Coleus Verschaffeltii, sixteen inches apart ; fifth, Caladium Esculentum, a foot and a half apart; sixth, Abutilon Thompsonii, fifteen inches apart ; the centre was planted with large Cannas, intermixed with Gladiolus. This bed was exceedingly beautiful for months. It will be noticed that the tallest plants occupied the center, while each circle toward the edge contained plants of less height. Where smaller beds are desired, a less number of circles or lines will be necessary ; one might be made with a large scarlet Geranium, Gladiolus or double Zinnias, for the centre, with white Feverfew, Centaurea or white Phlox Drummondii next, and surrounding these, Larkspur, Heliotrope, or other blue flowers, with yellow Calceolaria or Dwarf Nasturtium next, and outside of all plant a circle of Variegated Thyme, Sweet Alyssum, Mignonette, or other low-growing plant. A very pretty long ribbon bed is made by taking different colors of the same flower, like Phlox Drummondii, Portulaca, Verbenas, Stocks, and others described as being suitable. With a little care in studying descriptions, and a little experience, the work of arranging these beds becomes easy, pleasant and interesting.

Planting Mixed Borders and Beds.—A very common arrangement of flower beds consists in making borders along the walks, four, five or more feet wide; large beds in the lawn or separate, or a centre bed in the vegetable garden, and planting promiscuously with a general variety of all kinds and seasons of flowering. Be careful at planting time to place the tallest growers, such as Hollyhocks, Ricinus, Dahlias, etc., in the background of the border beds, or in the center of beds surrounded by walks, else they might hide some smaller growths. Where it is possible, plants and flowers of contrasting colors should be set to show to the best advantage, and those flowering at different times, to make the display continual throughout. Fig. 14 illustrates a plan for flower beds in a walk bordered with shrubbery.

Fig. 14. Flower Beds in Walk.

Flower Beds for Constant Cutting.-It never seems right to see beds that were planted principally for the adornment of the grounds and garden, robbed daily of young, fresh flowers for the table, bouquets, or to cut for friends. It is much better to have a bed or mixed border near at hand planted with free blooming varieties that are desirable for fragrance and brilliant colors, especially for this purpose. These will bloom all the more constant for having the young flowers cut as fast as they open, and it is surprising to see the amount of flowers that can daily be cut from quite a small bed. Such a bed should be planted largely with annual Phlox Drummondii, Sweet Pea, Zinnia, Stocks, Candytuft, Mignonette, besides Heliotrope, monthly Roses, Gladiolus, Dahlia, Geranium, Verbena, Pansy and others. An abundance of green should also be provided for, as foliage is an important item in all floral arrangements, a matter which is too frequently overlooked by both amateur and commercial florists. Nothing can be cultivated to supply this better than Shrubland Pet and the Rose Scented Geraniums, two varieties of this valuable family of plants that are easily propagated by every one, and which grow with great vigor if taken from the pots and planted in fertile soil. A few plants of each will afford a large supply of delightful green foliage, unequalled in the first named variety, for its beautiful dense foliage and many clusters of brilliant crimson flowers all summer, and in the latter for the agreeable, refreshing fragrance of the foliage, which is also of a deep green color and of beautiful form. There are several varieties of so-called Rose Geraniums, all differing somewhat in fragrance and appearance, most of which are vastly inferior, in all important respects, to the true rose-scented variety. Then, some plants, with beautiful foliage, such as Abutilon Thompsonii, Centaurea Gymnocarpa or the Achryanthes, Amaranthus, etc., should not be everlooked. These will furnish a variation of material for intermixing with and edging flowers in bouquets, baskets, and other arrangements, that is very desirable along with green. Smilax is a plant with finer green foliage than the Geraniums alluded to, but it is not so good for constant daily cutting, being a climber, and hardly available until it has made a growth of from three to six feet, as the vine with leaves attached are too succulent for use, with less than several months' age. Another plant deserving of more general cultivation, and valuable for this purpose, is Lemon Verbena (*Aloysia Citriodora*), which is of easy culture, and is a favorite wherever its delightful fragrance and delicate form of leaf are known.

The Soil: Its Preparation and Treatment.

—If we would be successful in cultivating flowers under any circumstances, it is of the greatest importance that we give our plants a deep, fertile and well drained soil to grow in. That attempts at floriculture may be shrouded in irremediable failures from other causes is possible ; but I freely assert that lack of attention to thoroughly securing these requisites is the direct cause of nearly every failure to produce fine flowers in abundance. This should be understood by beginners. Not a season passes but in July, August and September, flower beds are to be seen which were laid out and planted with much taste and expense perhaps, that contain at this season, only poor, unthrifty, flowerless plants, an eye-sore to the beholder, and a testimonial to the one fact, that the soil was unsuitably prepared for flowers. Few soils are so stubborn that with perfect drainage, either natural or artificial—and this if well done once will last a lifetime—with being trenched eighteen inches or two feet deep, and annually supplied with a dressing of manure, together with being well tilled, will not produce flowers in abundance.

Trenching is an operation which consists in working the soil to a great depth, with the use of the spade. It serves to promote the growth of vegetation, by giving to the roots ample

Fig. 15. Trenching

room for extension ; besides, with retaining moisture the entire depth to which the soil is stirred and broken, it prevents injury to plants in severe drouths, where they might be effected by drying, were the soil only worked to a shallow depth. In ordinary culture the surface soil, only, is overturned or stirred by the plough or spade, leaving the subsoil underneath, which is usually hard and compact, untouched ; but with trenching the operation is conducted to work up the latter as well as the former, keeping each part by itself, the surface soil above and the subsoil, which is of a sterile nature underneath. The annexed cut, representing a section of soil to be trenched, shows how this is accomplished. The surface soil shown in section *A*, to the width of about six feet across the bed, is first thrown out entirely and the subsoil underneath (*a*) is turned with the spade, moving it only enough to facilitate the work ; a section of surface soil about four feet wide, represented in the cut by *B*, is next thrown over in the space *A*, on subsoil *a*, and the subsoil now turned to light is overturned in like manner as that represented by *a* was. The soil in section *C*, to the width of about four feet, is in turn thrown into space *B*, and the subsoil underneath is overturned. The operation is continued in the same manner across the bed or lot, and the opening remaining at the end after the other side has been reached, can be filled up with the surface soil first thrown out.

Manure should be applied to flower beds in the fall, after severe frosts have finally cut down the plants, and annual bulbs and tubers are removed. Spread evenly over the surface, and incorporate well with the soil by spading it thorough and deep. Always have a supply of manure in some corner for such purposes. Those who keep a cow or horse will of course have enough. If you manage to have it six or twelve months old before using, it is best, although some fresher from the stable will answer the purpose. Those who cannot get manure readily should make a compost heap by gathering up a store of leaves in the fall and leaving them lay until spring, when they should be piled up in alternate layers with a cartload of sods from some meadow or roadside to rot, giving the heap a weekly soaking of soapsuds on washing days. Throw on, during the summer months, rakings and scrapings from the garden, and once in a while add a shovelful of lime, and a barrow load of black earth from the street, and by early winter you will have a mound of rich, black, crumbly loam, of fine fertilizing quality.

Where hardy plants, shrubs, or Roses that remain in the ground from year to year, are growing in the beds, care should be taken not to cut or spade so near them as to injure the roots at the annual fall spading. These are benefited by receiving a dressing of strawy manure, over their roots, late in the season, which should be raked off again in the spring. In spring the beds are to be worked over again with the spade, or digging-fork. If the manure worked in, in the fall, appears to have been ample, none need now be applied. We take exception, however, to new beds to be planted for the first time ; better give these another moderate dressing before spading. In no case do spading in the spring until the soil is dry. Imprudence in this respect will cause most land to become rough and cloddy, which cannot be remedied during that season. After nicely raking up the beds, always leaving the middle slightly elevated, you can carry out your plans—which should have been perfected before planting time—by setting out the hardiest plants first, finishing with the more tender kinds in May.

Sowing Seeds.

—Some flower seeds, like those of Candytuft, Convolvulus, Escholtzia, Larkspur, Mignonette, Poppy, Portulaca, Sweet Pea, etc., do better to sow directly where they are to bloom. As soon as the ground becomes warm and friable, say in April and

May, open drills—not too deep—and drop in the seed ; draw in fine earth and beat it down a little with the hoe or spade. Where whole or parts of beds are sown with a single kind of seed, they may be scattered broadcast, covering with light sandy soil, sprinkled on with the hand or through a fine sieve, or a slight raking will answer the same purpose. Never cover seeds of any kind too deep. Failures often arise from this cause alone. I consider the old rule of covering twice the depth of their own diameter to be reliable, and applicable to any kind of sowing. As soon as seedlings have made a second growth of leaves, they should be thinned to a distance which will give each plant space sufficient to develop in size. Pansies, Hollyhocks, Delphiniums and a few others, by sowing in August and September, will flower the next year, and earlier than if their sowing is deferred until spring. These should be slightly covered at the approach of cold weather. For further remarks on time of sowing various seeds in the open ground, see Weekly Classification of Work for May, June, July, August and September.

Most other seed-grown plants, besides those named above, are benefited by being transplanted, and should be started in a prepared seed-bed, cold-frame, hot-bed, or a box in the house. In either case, a rich, light, sandy loam should be used, as with plants intended for removal when they have attained a certain size, an abundance of fibrous roots is of importance, which can never be obtained if the seedlings are brought forward in a soil of a hard "bakey" character. Decomposed grass sods from a sandy meadow make excellent soil for this purpose.

Hot-Beds, Cold-Frames and Seed-Beds.

—Every family possessing a garden ought to have a hot-bed, even if it be only small, in which to start their seedling plants, Dahlia roots, Tuberose bulbs, etc., and also to root cuttings. Tender annuals and vegetables of all kinds for planting could be had three or four weeks earlier than if the seeds were sown in the open ground, thus advancing their season of maturity materially. A hot-bed is made by form-

ing a pile of fresh strawy horse manure some three feet in height, slightly elevated at what is to be the back end of the bed. As a number of loads will be required for an ordinary sized bed, it may be necessary to gather up manure for the purpose for some time previous to using it, in which case the accumulations should be kept from the wet under cover, and be frequently overturned to check its heating before needed. The bed may be sunk a foot or eighteen inches in the ground, if drained, and should be a foot larger each way than the frame which is to be used. The

Fig. 16.—Hot Bed.

manure should be well trodden down to prevent settling when finished. Lying thus causes it to ferment, which fermentation produces the lasting bottom heat that warms the soil and renders the bed essentially a miniature greenhouse. After the manure is in shape, the frame, which should be made of 1¼ or 1½ inch plank 18 inches wide, can be placed on at once and filled in with about four or five inches of light soil well enriched with fine manure. Banking up over the projecting portion of the manure on the outside with ground, will tend to confine the heat to the inside of the frame, and will also improve the appearance of the bed by hiding the manure. Keep the sash closed until the heat has warmed the soil well. Then better wait a day or two before sowing the seed. I prefer sowing in drills, about two or three inches apart, running across the bed. Care, however, is required in clear weather to prevent the heat rising to an injurious temperature. Abundant air should be given when the sun shines, by moving the sash up or down. The safest way is to be governed by a thermometer, which should be placed where the sun's rays will not strike it ; keep the temperature as near sixty degrees in the shade as possible. When the mercury indicates higher than that point, give air ; when below —as it will in frosty nights—cover with mats. By being attentive in this matter, seeds that were sown in April will have become thrifty, well-tempered plants by the latter part of May.

The principal advantages of a hot-bed may be secured by what is called a *Cold-Frame.* This is formed without manure, by placing the hot-bed frame upon a bed of soil in some sheltered place in the garden, protected from cold winds. Do not start the cold-frame until the latter part of April in this latitude, as we depend wholly on the sun for heating it. It requires much the same care with reference to airing on sunny days, and protecting with mats in cold nights, as does the hot-bed. Both should be watered occasionally when the soil demands it.

Many readers of the FLORIST can have neither of these conveniences. By starting a week or two later, seeds may be sown in a bed of good, mellow soil, made in some warm, sunny spot about the house, with good results. On the east or south side of a building is just the place, where the sun's rays reflected on the building, causes the bed to be some degrees warmer, consequently earlier than if made out in an open space. I will here remark, that all seeds come up sooner for having the ground shaded with shutters, mats, or perhaps, better than all, paper, until the shoots have reached the surface, when the covering must be removed at once.

Transplanting.

—I prefer to transplant seedling plants with a dibble or pointed stick, and pot grown plants with a garden trowel, just before or after a shower. Sometimes transplanting must be done in a dry spell. The best way then, is to plant carefully towards evening of the day, leaving a depression in the soil around each plant, which should be filled with water and allowed to settle away until the soil is thoroughly saturated. Next morning the earth should be drawn in, to prevent the wet soil from baking.

Summer Culture.—In summer the earth between the plants should be frequently stirred, after each rain at least. Some things, like Double Geraniums and Carnations, it is well to mulch with straw. Beds are better if calculated so that flowers or plants can be reached without treading on the ground.

The flowering season of many things, like Verbenas, Geraniums and Dahlias, may be lengthened, almost every autumn, by covering the plants with mats, etc., on cool nights to protect from the first September frosts. After some quite sharp frosts the weather usually comes off warm and pleasant for some time yet, and it is well to have the benefit of this on the plants.

Preparatory Treatment of Plants designed for Winter Flowering.— It should be borne in mind that in winter the natural conditions of heat, sunlight, and the lessened length of daylight, are adverse to the profuse growth of vegetation, and particularly the production of flower buds ; for this reason, it is of the *greatest importance* in plant culture, at this season, either in the dwelling or conservatory, to have, at the outset, good plants of strong vitality. When plants pass into the winter quarters in a weakened condition, from any cause, they will be apt to remain weak all winter. The best way of securing plants for winter flowering, especially rapid growing kinds, is to start with young plants the spring previous, and prepare them for this purpose during the summer, by giving them a favorable opportunity for making a healthy growth in the open air, either in pots plunged to their rims in soil, refuse hops or other material, or by being bedded out, and during this time, and until within a month or two of cold weather, practice a system of heading them in to cause a compact stocky growth, and also to prevent the exhaustion of plant force by flowering, which, if allowed, would be detrimental to the crop in winter. For special remarks on the culture of all suitable varieties, see the directions accompanying each kind.

The plants that were bedded during summer, such as Carnations, Violets, etc., should be taken up and potted as early as the first two weeks of September, in order that they may fully recover from the effects of the operation before cold weather sets in. With plants grown for the beauty of their foliage, it is needless to adopt this course of summer treatment, further than to have them healthy and of fine form, whether they be large or small. Some small pots, containing pretty plants, placed among the larger ones of a collection will enhance appearances greatly. In the fall avoid taking plants into their winter quarters too soon, but gradually inure them to the confined air of the room or bay window, by keeping them inside during cold nights or cool weather, allowing them to be fully exposed to the air in partial shade, as under the piazza, or at the side of the house, during fine weather. In the case of having a conservatory for the plants they may be placed in it at once, but an abundance of air should be allowed to circulate through the structure at all times when the temperature will allow. The plants grown in pots should receive their final shift into the pots or boxes they are to occupy during winter, in September or October. We find that a soil made of two or three parts of decomposed turf and one part of well rotted stable manure, with the addition of a little clean sand, is suited to nearly every plant grown, and is better than "chip ground," so commonly used.

Watering Plants, the Lawn, etc., in Summer.—Whenever it becomes necessary to resort to watering in dry weather, it is much better to apply sufficient water to thoroughly soak the soil while about it, than to apply a small quantity day by day, a custom very prevalent among cultivators. When about to water plants first draw the soil away from the base of the stalk in order to form a sort of basin in which to pour the water ; fill this up and let it settle away repeatedly until a sufficiency has been applied, then draw the earth again to the plant, which will prevent the soil from becoming baked by the sun. A thorough watering in this manner ought to last for several weeks in the driest time of summer. When entire beds are to be watered the soil should be opened by thrusting a digging-fork into it in numerous places before sprinkling ; then the beds should be passed over again and again with the pot and sprinkler until a sufficiency has been absorbed. The next day the surface of the bed should be mellowed up with the rake or hoe.

This rule of thoroughly watering each time water is needed, and then not again until it is really necessary, applies quite as well to watering plants in pots at all seasons of the year, either out of doors or in the house and conservatory, as in the open ground. Do not over-water pot plants, however, as it is contrary to the nature of the generality of plants to thrive in soil in such a condition.

Autumn Planting of Hyacinths, Tulips and other Hardy Bulbs.— Were the Bulbs which are known as Hardy or Dutch Bulbs grown by planting in the spring time of the year with the Gladiolus, Tigridia, etc., their culture would be more common, and collections of the choicer varieties, such as are conspicuous for their beauty and grandeur, would be less rare. Planting at the approach of winter is rather contrary to the general rule of garden management, and we are inclined to neglect this only means for securing the flowering of Hyacinths, Tulips, Crocus, etc., early the following spring, or for improving the collections that may be growing in our gardens, which consist far too often of inferior varieties, considering the trifling outlay which is necessary for obtaining a better quality of stock.

The planting of these may be done at any time during the months of September, October and November, or even later, provided the ground remain unfrozen later, which is sometimes the case. To be entirely safe it is best, perhaps, not to defer the work much after October. Bulbs will succeed in any good garden soil; in order, however, to secure the highest degree of success in their culture, it is necessary to plant in a soil that is well drained and enriched with thoroughly decayed manure. When all plantings have been completed, and before winter sets in, cover the beds with several inches of leaves, straw or other coarse litter, to prevent the severe action of freezing from injuring the Bulbs. In situations much exposed to the wind, a few brush or sticks thrown on will prevent its being blown off. Early in the spring this fall covering should be removed. Where beds planted with hardy spring-flowering Bulbs are required for summer flowers, Hyacinths, Tulips, etc., may safely be taken up to prepare for planting the subsequent fall, as early as two weeks after the flowers have disappeared, provided the precaution of covering the Bulbs with soil, to allow the foliage to become gradually ripened, is observed.

Taking up Plants from the open ground in the Fall.—Many kinds of bedding plants, such as Geraniums, Veronicas, Stocks, Salvias, Ageratums, Roses, Carnations, etc., can be taken up from the flower-beds at the approach of frosts, and transferred into pots, or even packed thickly in boxes of soil, by taking care to have some earth adhering to the roots, and by keeping in a rather dry and cool cellar, or better yet in a cold pit through the winter. It must, however, be done at the sacrifice of much autumnal beauty, as they require a severe cutting back of at least one-third or one-half of the shoots. But this is gain after all, for such plants, when kept over, in most cases, make a better show the next year than the plants of the present season's striking. They may receive one thorough watering when potted; after which they should be kept quite dry until spring, when water should be applied every few days in increased quantities as they commence making a new growth.

SIMPLE INSTRUCTIONS FOR PROPAGATING FROM CUTTINGS AND LAYERS.

The larger proportion of plants that do not seed freely, if at all, or which cannot be increased by division of the roots, may be propagated from cuttings or layers of the young growing shoots. How important a thorough understanding of these methods of propagation is to the florist, may be comprehended when we consider that this is about the only, and really the best, means of increasing the majority of that class of plants commonly known as perennial greenhouse and bedding plants, in which may be included Tender and Hardy Roses, Geraniums, Fuchsias, Carnations, Verbenas, Heliotropes, and very many others of equal importance as decorative plants. As the two methods are quite distinct, I shall treat upon each separately, commencing with that of propagating from cuttings, as this is the more commonly employed method of the two.

The principal conditions essential to successfully propagate from cuttings are nearly the same with all plants susceptible of being perpetuated by this means. These are first, that the cutting be in a proper condition; second, that it be rightly pruned or trimmed; third, that it receive suitable treatment and care while rooting; and fourth, that after it is rooted it be transplanted from the cutting box or bed to soil at the right time, and that it be properly attended to until it becomes a well established plant.

With the generality of kinds the ends of newly formed shoots make the best cuttings, and are greatly preferable to old hardened growth. There is a certain time and condition in the growth of all plant shoots in which, if a cutting be taken, it will strike root and make a plant sooner and better than at any other time. To ascertain this condition, and how far back it extends from the growing terminal bud, it should be understood that there are different degrees of hardness present in the wood—the youngest part being the softest, while towards the base of the shoot it is harder and more fibrous as the oldest portion is reached. By taking a cutting off, down in this hardened portion of the shoot, it would be found to root slowly, and in some plants not at all, and at best would make a plant, comparatively, of inferior quality; while with adopting the opposite extreme, making a short cutting of the succulent young growth only, it would be still less likely to root, and instead would, perhaps, quickly decay. Now the right place to cut or break it off (breaking is generally practiced by florists) is at the furthest point in from the end *where a condition can be found that is somewhat hardened, and yet sufficiently brittle or crisp, that it will snap off with a clean break,* instead of bending without breaking, or of parting with a rough break in which the fibers of the bark portion, or perhaps the whole, will protrude, showing them to have become hardened and tough. Practice will demonstrate that in the difference of one joint there is considerable variation in the hardness of the growth; it is always better to break or cut at a point which is rather soft than at one that has become too hard. Experience will put the careful operator in the way of determining the right place with scarcely a failure.

To rightly prune or trim a cutting it is required that the superfluous leaves and leaf stalks be removed, and that the base be cut away with a sharp knife. Cuttings of some plants will callus and form roots at the base, no matter whether it be just below a leaf joint or not, while others seem to root best from the leaf joints, and these should accordingly be cut off just below. It would be best, perhaps, for amateurs to cut all below a joint, as with limited experience they have little opportunity for ascertaining which varieties do, and which do not, require it. Fig. 17 represents a Geranium shoot as taken from the plant, and also a cutting ready for striking made from it. A point below the joint of the fourth leaf, counting from above, was found in suitable condition for the lower part of the cutting, and here the cut was made close

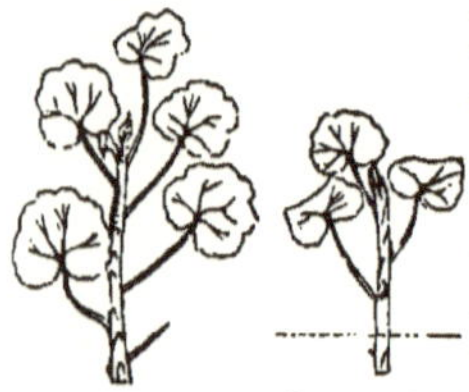

Fig. 17. *Branch and Cutting of Geranium.*

up to the joint. The fourth leaf was removed, and also parts of the largest remaining leaves were cut away to admit air and light to the cutting, which is especially necessary where many are put in close together ; this cutting away the tips is well with all varieties having large leaves, as it also prevents an unnecessary absorption of moisture from the material in which the cutting is placed to root.

Clean sand is the material usually preferred in which to strike cuttings. Whether placed in a propagating house where, in cool or cold weather, the sand may be heated from the bottom, to be fifteen degrees warmer than the air in the house, or in a box or pan in the dwelling or garden, it should be about three inches deep, and be underlaid by broken pots or other material to allow for the escape of an excess of water which it may chance to receive occasionally. According to their size, cuttings may be put into the sand at various depths and distances apart, but seldom deeper than an inch for long-jointed cuttings, or less than a third or half inch for small ones, and at such a distance that the leaf points of the different ones just touch each other ; water thoroughly when the cuttings are first set, and then daily or every other day as they require it, only guarding against allowing the surface to become dry. A bright, sunny place in the window, where some air can be admitted, is the best place for the cutting box, but whenever the sun shines, shade them by laying a paper over them. The " saucer " system of propagating plants is a very excellent one for amateurs to practice. It consists of placing the cuttings very close together in a water-tight saucer or dish containing several inches of sand, and then keeping the sand thoroughly saturated with water until the cuttings are rooted. There is not the least necessity of shading the cuttings from the sun, and the saucers may be keep constantly in its full glare, provided sufficient water is at all times present.

From one to three or four weeks is the required time for cuttings to root, depending somewhat upon the condition of the cutting and treatment received, but principally upon the difference in kinds, some rooting much sooner than others. It is better to pot them off as soon as the roots are a fourth or even an eighth of an inch long, than to wait until they become an inch or two long, which endangers their being broken off ; when it is supposed that nearly sufficient time has ensued for them to root, their state may be ascertained by drawing one out for examination, which can be replaced again. Callusing always directly precedes the formation of roots ; this is an irregular growth which forms upon the base or along the side of a cutting, and its presence is a healthy sign that roots will soon appear. After the cuttings have been potted off, much the same care should be given them, as regards shading and watering, as they received in the cutting bed, for a week, or until the roots have started into growth in the soil. Never put the most common plant in a dirty pot. Never fill a pot so full of soil but that it may receive and hold water enough to go through ; every pot should have half an inch of vacancy above the soil. A frost which could not reach the roots of a pot plant that is plunged in earth to the rim, may destroy all the fibres of even a hardy one if the pot be exposed.

Some plants, such as Carnations, Roses and many of the hardy shrubs, are best propagated by layering, especially if there is no convenience of a good greenhouse propagating bed at hand.

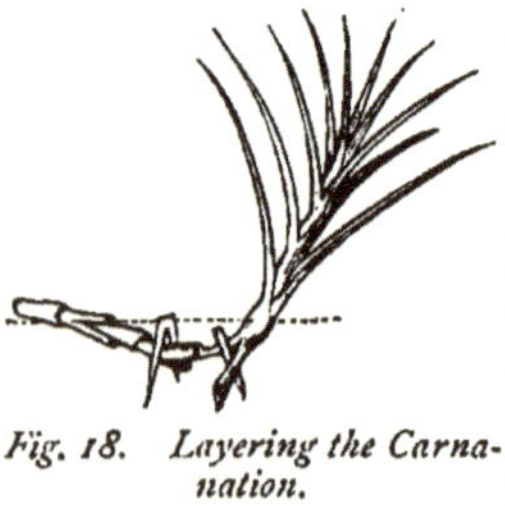

Fig. 18. *Layering the Carnation.*

Layering consists in bending and fastening a growing branch into a slight depression at the side of the plant, covering a portion of it from which it is to throw roots, and allowing the growing extremity to extend out of the soil to form a new plant. In preparing the layer, at the lowest point of the bend an oblique cut is made from the under side, about half or two-thirds way through the branch. This is done for the purpose of preventing the free return of the sap to the plant, which greatly promotes the formation of roots. Fig. 18 represents a Carnation branch prepared for layering. To keep a layer firmly in its place it should be pegged down as shown in the cut. A small bit of wood or other substance should also be inserted in the cut to keep it open that it may not grow together. The separation from the parent plant is not effected till the layer is sufficiently provided with roots, which will usually be in from six to twelve weeks, although layers of some plants require a year or two to become rooted, but these are hardly in the line of plants which amateurs propagate.

HANGING BASKETS AND GARDEN VASES.

Fig. 19. A Hanging Basket of Plants.

The plants of drooping, trailing and climbing habits are, with scarcely an exception, of easy growth, and always interesting and attractive, if planted where their peculiar growth can be accommodated. The proper situations are afforded by hanging baskets and garden vases, which, with judicious planting, form very effective means of adornment. Hanging baskets are becoming very popular, because they are so easily given a place where they will thrive,—accommodating themselves to positions such as being suspended from a piazza or tree, or a trellis on the side of a house or in front of a window afford, thus enabling thousands of plant admirers to possess a luxuriant growth of plants, and also flowers, who for want of a garden would be deprived of the pleasure. Another recommendation to their general introduction, is their slight cost, which, indeed, need be very little aside of the cost of necessary plants, where a person possesses any skill at construction. A piece of strong wire, shaped and fastened into a circle, and several yards of lighter wire attached to it and woven into a sort of basket or dish-shaped structure, which, with being moss-lined, will answer for holding soil, is all that is necessary for producing the most beautiful effect. The manufactured earthen hanging pots, rustic and wire baskets, if of tasty design, are beautiful for this purpose, but where their expense might be an objection, such a home-made basket will do quite well. Persons unacquainted with plants and selecting for this purpose should discriminate between droopers or trailers and climbers, and the upright growing plants which are to be used as "body" to the display, such as Begonia, Centaurea, Geranium, Cuphea, etc. By carefully reading descriptions you will scarcely fail to make a suitable selection. I will suggest that it is scarcely possible to stock a hanging basket, much less a garden vase, with plants grown from seed, as seventy-five or even more out of every hundred cultivators who have made the attempt could testify. The trouble is, that seed-grown plants cannot be reared strong enough by spring to make any show; besides only a few are suitable, Sweet Alyssum, Thunbergia, Petunia and Maurandia being the best that can be recommended and these should be sown very early.

For adorning the lawn, the terrace or the garden, nothing can be finer than a vase of chaste design, made of iron, stone or earthenware, and planted with droopers around the edge, and Geraniums, Heliotropes, Abutilons, Fuchsias, Caladiums, Cannas, or other attractive flowering and showy plants in the center. Vases are usually somewhat costly, being manufactured from expensive material, but by removing them into a shed or outhouse at the approach of winter they may do service for a lifetime, on which account they are not so expensive after all. Many people prefer a rustic vase to any other kind; these need not be costly, as they are readily made in winter with the use of a few tools, from material procured from the woods.

Culture and Treatment.—The culture of vases and hanging baskets is nearly identical. I desire to impress upon the minds of those who have their care in hand, the importance of supplying them with an abundance of water at all times; especially during hot weather, water should be poured on them in sufficient quantity to *thoroughly moisten every portion of soil* every time it is required. This is about the only matter in which vases and baskets

2

need attention, after once established, and the difference between their being well grown or poorly grown, nine times out of ten, may be directly ascribed to the amount of attention or neglect they receive in this respect. (Temperature 32°, 45°, 80°, except where noted or elsewhere described.)

Fig. 20.   Tradescanthia Repens Vittata.

Select List of Trailers Suitable for Baskets, Vases, Trellises, etc.

Alternantheras. See description of varieties in general list of plants.
Coliseum Ivy, a rapid growing drooper, forming a dense mass of long, dark green foliage.
Deeringia Variegata, a beautiful variegated plant of climbing habit. (35°, 50°, 80°.)
Ficus Repens, an admirable climbing or drooping plant for baskets, etc., having small, almost round leaves, and wiry stems; distinct and beautiful. (40°, 50°, 80°.)
Gazanias. See description of varieties in general list of plants.
Geraniums. See description of Ivy-leaf section in special article.
German Ivy (Senecio Mikanoides), not an ivy at all, but so-called because of its ivy-shaped leaves; one of our most rapid growing climbers, always healthy, beautiful and attractive; very desirable. (33°, 45°, 75°.)
Isolepsis Gracilis, one of the grasses, forming a dense plant of gracefully drooping round blades of lively green color, each bearing a small tuft-like bud at its end. (35°, 50°, 90°.)
Ivies. See description of varieties in the article on Ivies.
Lobelias, exceedingly valuable droopers; see description of varieties in general list of plants.
Lonicera Aurea Reticulata, a pretty climber; the foliage is distinctly reticulated or netted with gold upon green; very desirable for trellis culture; the root is hardy, with slight protection.
Lophosphernum Scandens, a climber, with attractive heart-shaped foliage. (34°, 50°, 80°.)
Maderia Vine, well-known as an excellent climber for both summer and winter culture, with beautiful thick glossy foliage; excellent to train up the window and for trellis; a tuberous plant, very easily grown. The dry tuber should be kept in a warm, dry place in winter. (For forcing, 34°, 50°, 90°.)
Mahernia Odorata, a beautiful plant, with finely cut foliage, covered in spring with very many sweet-scented, bright yellow flowers, of bell shape; excellent in pots. (34°, 50°, 75°.)
Maurandia Barclayana, a superb climber, of rapid dense growth, producing many flowers of foxglove shape; among the best of plants for covering trellises in the open ground. It is readily grown from seed, which should be sown early. (34°, 50°, 75°.)
Mesembryanthemums. See description of varieties in general list of plants.
Mimulus Moschatus, the Musk Plant, the leaves of which emit a genuine, yet delicate, musky odor; of compact, drooping habit; very attractive as a pot plant. It can be propagated either from seed, cuttings, or by division of the roots in the spring. The plant may be kept in a half dormant state during winter. (This and the following, 34°, 45°, 89°.)
Mimulus triginoides, a variety producing exceedingly beautiful golden and orange flowers of tubular shape, with the richest maroon spots and blotches. Both delight in moisture.
Moneyvine (Lysimachia nummelaria), one of our most valuable droopers, has handsome dark green, chain-like foliage; its rapid growing shoots will fall over the edge of a vase or basket, and grow to the length of three or more feet; flowers beautifully in June.
Moneyvine, Golden (L. nummelaria aurea). This is a new variety, quite similar to the above, in form of foliage and habit, but the color of the leaves is nearly golden yellow; not so rapid a grower; I have not tested its hardiness, but presume it will stand the winter unprotected.

Poa trivalis, another fine grass, with narrow white and green variegated leaves. (40°, 60°, 80°.)
Saxifraga Sarmentosa (Strawberry Geranium), a running strawberry-like plant of curious and
    interesting growth, with striped and mottled foliage; very valuable.
Torrenia Asiatica, a pretty drooping plant; will not bear much cold; flowers blue, of lovely
    tint and shape, and extremely beautiful; excellent for pot culture. (40°, 60°, 80°.)
Tradescanthia Vulgaris (Joint Plant—Wandering Jew), an old-fashioned drooper, of the easiest
    culture, with beautiful dark glossy foliage. It is quite certain of giving satisfaction.
Tradescanthia Repens Vittata. (See Fig. 20.) This is a Tradescanthia of comparative
    recent origin, and is generally considered to be the most beautiful of all the varieties of
    this desirable family of plants. The leaves are beautifully variegated, as shown in the
    engraving; the stripes, which are of a clear, waxy white and whitish yellow color, on bright,
    glossy green ground, extend the entire length of the leaf usually. Like all Tradescanthias,
    it is particularly recommendable for home cultivation either in baskets or pots, as it will
    thrive in a temperature either high or low, in a moist atmosphere or in desert dryness, and
    is not at all particular as regards light, in this respect being almost equal to the Ivy.
Tradescanthia Zebrina, a variety with finely striped green and reddish leaves.
Variegated Thyme, very desirable as a drooper and bedder, the foliage being distinctly variegated.
Vinca minor variegata, one of the best and most attractive droopers in cultivation; the leaves
    are from one to two inches in diameter, and distinctly variegated; a rapid grower.
Other suitable varieties are described throughout the general list.

PLANT CULTURE IN AND ABOUT THE HOUSE.

Among the readers of the HOME FLORIST will be those whose surroundings restrict them to
engage only in cultivating plants in and about the house, converting a sunny or bay window
into a green-house in winter, and moving their plant stand under the veranda, or into the open

Fig. 21.   Open-Air Window Box.

air when warm weather approaches. This,
with the planting of an outside window box in
summer, the growing of hanging baskets (see
article on Hanging Baskets and Garden Vases),
Ferneries, or Wardian cases, and Ivies for permanent it might be added, are about the limit to
which they can indulge in such decorations. It
is, however, a pleasure to know that with these
a beautiful show of plants and flowers may be
maintained continually throughout the year,
with little trouble and expense.

Open-Air Window Boxes.—Fig. 21
is an illustration of this ready means of growing plants and flowers, which is adapted for
ornamenting the windows of any room, either
inside or outside, be it in the first or fifth
story of a building, as some living rooms are in
the city. These are boxes made to fit the win-
dow-casing or sill, and planted with Scarlet
Geranium, Mignonette, the pretty blue Lobelia, Verbena, and even Roses, etc. Morning
Glory, Ivy, Maderia Vine, or other climbers
are planted at the ends of the box, to be
trained on wires up and around the windows.
Very beautiful.

Plant Culture in Winter.—To learn
what can be done at plant forcing in winter,
under favorable circumstances, it is only necessary to witness the extensive crop of flowers in
large variety that are daily cut, and also the
beautiful foliage plants grown at this season, in
the commercial greenhouses of all large American cities and towns; and, although I would
not encourage the thought, that plants can be grown to an equal degree of perfection in the
dwelling as in the florist's well appointed structures, yet very satisfactory results can be obtained
by nearly every one if the matter is properly entered upon and executed, and beautiful, vigorous,
blooming plants be the result. Sometimes those whose efforts in growing plants and
flowers in the open air in summer are bountifully rewarded, find vexations disappointments
attending similar undertakings in winter greatly to their surprise. Unquestionably, the
cause of this lies more frequently in the fact that the necessary course of treatment is not sufficiently understood, than that the conditions of light, heat, etc., which the dwelling affords, are

unfavorable to plant life. These latter conditions have their marked influence on growth it is true, but, then, the adaptability of plants is so varied, that at least several varieties may be employed, which will thrive under any circumstances, that are likely to exist in our dwellings. In " Open-Air Floriculture " are given directions for preparing plants for winter flowering.

The Winter Quarters.—Next to a conservatory, built expressly for plants, a bay window, off from the living room, and from which it will receive sufficient warmth, is the best place for cultivating plants in winter, although a window facing east, south or west, answers the purpose very well, and should we even be less fortunate and have only windows with northern exposure, where the sun in winter never strikes in, there is no need of being entirely deprived of the beauty of plants and flowers, because the Ivies, Begonias, Euonymus, Callas, Tradescanthias, Lobelias, Achryanthes, Centaureas, etc., and, perhaps, most important of all, the entire list of Hardy Bulbs, for flowers, all of which readily dispense with direct sunlight, will thrive beautifully here, provided the conditions of heat, air, moisture, etc., are correct. But these are essential to plant growth under any other circumstances as well.

Temperature, Selection of Suitable Plants, Protection, etc.—The amateur, who, for the first time perhaps, might desire to engage in the cultivation of plants in winter, would naturally be anxious to know, What plants can best be grown in my house? The answer to this question is easily arrived at by each of us, provided the temperature which can be maintained for the plants is known, and also the temperature in which the various plants suited to winter culture will best thrive. Recall to your mind the lowest temperature of previous seasons, as indicated by the thermometer, or if you were without this almost indispensable instrument, recollect whether it ever fell to 32°—the freezing point—and allow this knowledge to be your guide on the one hand, while for guidance in reference to making selections suited to your temperature, observe the figures and degrees in parenthesis following the names of the varieties described throughout this work as suitable for window culture. These figures indicate the *extremes of temperature*, both high and low, that each plant will bear, and also the degree most congenial to its growth, as a *night* temperature. To render this more clear, let us take as an instance the Abutilons, described on the 34th page. The descriptions and cultural directions of this family are preceded by (33, 45, 85°), which indicates that these plants will bear a temperature of 33° as one extreme and 85° as the other, for some time without injury, while 45° is best suited to the plant as a night temperature; ten to twenty-five degrees above this is to be considered nearest right for their growth in the daytime.

The various varieties of the Ivy family possess so many desirable qualities as house plants, and will thrive under such widely varying conditions, that they are recommendable to all cultivators as a class with which failure to cultivate successfully is scarcely possible.

It should be understood in this connection that plants can be safely kept through several additional degrees of cold than indicated by the *first* figure (lowest extreme) by protection, and it is safe to calculate somewhat on this for the few excessively severe nights of each winter, by giving the more tender ones especial attention at such times. Simply pinning several thicknesses of newspaper over a plant, as shown in the annexed cut, would protect it sufficiently for remaining a number of hours in a temperature from five to ten degrees lower than it would otherwise bear. Ordinarily where danger is apprehended from leaving plants next to the window, during severe nights, they can be moved to the middle or further side of the room, which is sure to be several degrees warmer. By setting them close together it is easy to protect the lot by spreading newspapers on them and throwing a blanket over all. To correct too high a temperature admit air from the outside.

Fig. 22.   Protection.

General Directions for Indoor Plant Management.—*Airing.*—As often as the weather, from its mildness, will allow of introducing air among the plants, from the outside, it should be done, but be careful to avoid a strong, direct draft of wind upon them. Cold, fresh air striking on Roses may bring on mildew. Maintain a temperature as nearly uniform as possible, endeavoring to keep it at a degree best suited to the majority of the plants in the collection, being guided in this respect by the figures in parenthesis throughout the descriptions.

Moisture and Watering.—One difficulty amateurs have to contend with in growing plants in the living room—especially if heated with anthracite coal stoves and ranges—is dryness of the atmosphere. This can in a measure be obviated by nailing a narrow strip of board on the front and back edges of the plant-stand shelves, or false bottom of the window sill, and filling up with three-fourths of an inch of sand, upon which the pots are to be placed; keep the sand quite wet. The moisture escaping is what counteracts the dryness of the air. It will improve appearances to cover the surface between the pots with moss. Sprinkle the foliage of plants occasionally, and whenever the surface of the earth shows signs of dryness, water so that the soil be saturated and no more. Too much water passing through impoverishes the soil in a short time, besides doing the plant no good. As a rule, never allow water to stand in the saucers as it tends to sour the earth.

Insects.—If any plants become infested with *Aphis* or *Green-fly*, take a handful of tobacco stems, steep in water until it looks like strong tea, and wash the affected foliage, or else fumigate the plants by burning tobacco stems. The presence of *Red Spider* indicates too dry an atmosphere. Any plants affected should, several times daily, receive a thorough sprinkling or washing with water. *Mealy Bug* and *Scale*, if they appear, may be exterminated by washing and brushing the affected part of the plant. To remove *Angle Worms*, plants should be tapped out of the pots and the worms picked from the ball of earth.

Pruning, etc.—Any tendency in plants to become irregular in shape or too tall, should be corrected by pinching. Unless it is desirable to have a showy window, as seen from the street, the pots should be turned frequently, to prevent the plants from growing towards the light.

Ferneries and Wardian Cases.—Lovers of plants and flowers should by no means overlook the advantages, presented by these novel and successful appliances, for growing plants in the dwelling in the autumn, winter and spring. Dryness of atmosphere and dust are among the detrimental influences which we meet in winter plant culture, but by adopting the Wardian case principle of growing plants, these are entirely avoided, and instead, a uniform moist atmosphere is secured, which is altogether congenial to plant growth, no matter how dry the air outside in the drawing room or parlor may be. A glass case or shade is the principal agent employed. This is placed over plants growing in a vase or stand, to which it is fitted, and completely surrounding the plants. It retains the moisture of the atmosphere, and constantly returns it to the bed, thus also making frequent watering unnecessary. Usually plants with striking foliage are employed in Fernery culture, the Ferns and Lycopodiums being especially prized for the purpose, although all mentioned in the descriptions, including the flowering Begonias, are

Fig. 23. Round Fernery.

Fig. 24. Square Fernery.

quite as suitable. After planting the Fernery, the only care necessary to its management is to prop up the glass on one side, or entirely remove it for a short time daily after the morning dusting, and decaying flowers or foliage should be removed. Water should be given only when the surface of the soil becomes dry, which will not be often.

Culture of Hyacinths and other Hardy Bulbs in Glasses, Pots, etc., for Winter Decoration.—Taking advantage of the peculiarity of these bulbs to grow and flower freely in any medium capable of retaining moisture, we find it easy, with a little forethought, to have a profusion of bloom in the house or conservatory during the winter, and the presence of their brilliant colors among the various pot plants is very desirable for adding to the attractiveness of the winter collection. Whether bulbs are grown in glasses of water or in pots, vases, or other articles, they should, in either case, to make a complete success of the undertaking, be removed after planting, to a cellar, or any cool, dark place, here to remain six or eight weeks, for the purpose of causing a growth of roots before the leaves and flower stems start into growth. From this place they can be brought directly into the parlor or conservatory where they are to flower. The difference of a week or two between the periods of starting will produce a corresponding difference in the periods of bloom. When growing Hyacinths or Crocus in the glasses made for the purpose, it is necessary to see that the base of the bulb, only, touches the water; also, after admitting to the light, the water should be changed occasionally. In pot, box or vase culture, bulbs should be planted one-third or one-half of their heights in the soil or other material employed, moderately pressing the same around the bulb and applying water sufficient to soak thoroughly before placing into the dark quarters above alluded to. Bulbous plants of any kind should never be allowed to suffer for lack of water while in a growing state. A very good course to pursue in managing bulbs in glasses, is by first starting them in clean sand in some cool place, and after they have become well rooted, transferring them to the glasses, first washing all sand from the roots. Dark colored glasses are preferable to clear ones for bulb culture. Any attempt at forcing the hardy bulbs will be quite certain of being attended with successful results, only take care that the temperature be not too high where they are to flower. The flowers will develop most beautifully in a rather cool place, where the thermometer, however, never falls to the freezing point, for, although a slight freeze will not destroy them, it will lessen the beauty of the flowers.

Fig. 25.

THE AMATEUR'S CONSERVATORY.

A well managed Plant Conservatory opening from the living room, and accessible at all times, is, perhaps, the most beautiful and ever-changing source of recreation that can be introduced in connection with the home, and in consideration of the attractive features it possesses is comparatively an inexpensive source of gratification, particularly if the duties connected with its management are discharged by the patrons of its innumerable stores of interest.

The subject of conservatories is, at the present time, comparatively new and undeveloped. This is especially true outside of our large cities, and doubtless many amateurs have given the subject of possessing one some consideration, only to finally drop it entirely with the belief that, however desirable this would be, the erection of one for a moderate amount, and the after management of it, would, in their case, be hardly practical, if not wholly impossible.

It is my desire to present, in the pages of the HOME FLORIST, such facts and suggestions relative to building, stocking and managing home conservatories as experience points out as being applicable to the wants of amateur florists, hoping by these means to remove erroneous impressions, and enable the reader to view the matter in a proper and practical light.

Utility of a Conservatory.—With the erection of a suitable structure, cut flowers for bouquets and other means of adornment can be grown quite as well in winter as in the open ground in summer, thus affording a continuous season of flowers; besides, all beautiful and rare plants may be grown of large size, and to greater perfection than is possible, without means of the perpetual growing state of atmosphere which should here exist, and young plants for the flower garden, hanging baskets and other purposes can be propagated and reared without additional expense, while vegetable and flower seeds of all kinds may be started into growth. These various last-named items, with the growing of flowers, which would otherwise be bought at the florist's greenhouses in winter, may be made to go far towards balancing the expense and investment account. Besides, in most small towns, where no regular florist is located, or in the rural districts, the home conservatory, aside of serving the purpose for which it was intended, might readily be made self-supporting, and more, if those who have the management in hand would desire to engage in growing a stock of plants and some extra hanging baskets, and offering them for sale at a reasonable price. They would be surprised to see how eagerly neighbors and friends would purchase all their surplus that could be spared, in the spring, when the plants would be in full vigor and flower. I also venture the assertion, that were more cut flowers and nice foliage grown in winter, than would be needed for home use, by making such fact known, a demand could easily be created for them at paying prices, to be used for bouquets and decorating at weddings, parties, etc. I make these suggestions in the belief that in thousands of vicinities throughout our country persons might combine profit with pleasure in cultivating plants and flowers in the conservatory with the most pleasing results. Ladies and young people, especially, would find this a pleasing and fascinating employment for spare moments, and one devoid of heavy or irksome toil.

Fig. 26.   End View of a Cheap Conservatory.

Plans and Approximate Cost.—Although conservatories that are erected in connection with the home are usually built in costly style, and to serve an ornamental purpose in an architectural sense, I would by no means have it inferred that a good one cannot be erected for quite a small sum of money. I can call to mind structures of this kind, on private places, that have cost various figures, from $2,000 or $3,000 each, down to $100 and less. One very simple structure, which is heated by an ordinary base-burning coal stove, and in which, at any time, can be seen a fine growth of plants, hanging baskets and flowers, has pleased me so much that I have had an engraving made of the ground plan (Fig. 27). The building is ten feet by twelve feet, and is seven feet to the rafters at the lower end it being a lean-to

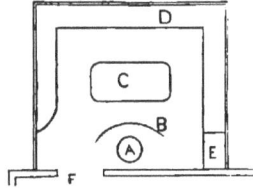

against the dwelling. The beds or benches are two and a half feet high, and nearly two feet wide. On the floor at the sides and ends of the aquarium, are placed tall plants, such as the side benches will not accommodate. In case an aquarium were not wanted, a plant bench might be built up a foot or more from the floor in its stead. The sides of the house from the benches upward are of glass, and the ventilators are fixed in the roof. The rafters support a number of fine growing hanging baskets and altogether the house is quite complete, and cost the owner, perhaps, inside of $60.

The large view shown of a conservatory, above Fig. 25, represents a house, size sixteen by twenty-four feet, the cost of which would be $700 and upwards, if heated in the most approved style, with hot water boiler, and one hundred and fifty to two hundred feet of four-inch cast iron pipe. The same sized house might, however, be built in plain, durable style, similar to Fig. 26, for about half that figure and be pre-

Fig. 27.   A Ground Plan.

A represents the coal stove; B, a screen placed at a height allowing the heat to strike underneath as well as over it; C, acquarium or plant bench; D, plant bench; E, water barrel or sink; F, entrance from dwelling.

cisely as valuable for plant growing, while by employing another means of heating, which is very extensively in use by florists, being much cheaper, namely, the brick furnace and flue, the cost might again be lessened $150, which would bring the entire cost down to $200, and perhaps even less, for quite a large-sized house. By building of smaller dimensions than sixteen by twenty-four feet the cost would be proportionately less. In a house like that represented in Fig. 25, the ventilators for admitting fresh air consist of the side sashes, of the raised portion of the roof; these are hung by hinges above, and are worked by means of pulleys or rods from the interior. The roof of Fig. 26 is built more simple, and consists of sashes, which reach from the plate board to the ridge piece. Every alternate sash serves the purpose of a ventilator, by being hinged on the plate or gutter board, and is raised or lowered by mean of a light iron bar eighteen inches long, with holes in, attached to the top of the sash, and which is secured to a nail in the ridge piece. Fig. 28 represents the cross section of this house, showing the internal arrangement of the beds and walks, and also the brick flues for heating, which are under the side beds. The walks should be two and a half to three feet wide, and extend from the dwelling entrance to the outside door on each side of the middle bed. A shows a cross section of bed in a house, heated by two four-inch hot water pipes. The brick furnace or the hot water boiler for heating, may be placed to be fed with fuel, from the basement of the dwelling.

In heating with a hot water boiler and pipes the heat is imparted to the atmosphere inside the structure by laying the pipes from the boiler in one continuous line throughout the building, under the beds, and returning to the boiler again. The smoke from the boiler may be conducted to the chimney of the dwelling. Through these pipes the water circulates, continually flowing from and returning into the boiler while the latter is heated. It becomes necessary to turn the course of the pipes at the corners, and at the extreme end by means of elbows, but this does not materially retard the circulation. With furnace and flue heating it is different; here the heat is distributed directly from the latter, which is built to pass nearly around the house, under the side beds, with a gradual ascent the entire distance, to give draft, opening into a chimney built at the side of the conservatory near the house end. At the outside door it will be necessary to cover the pipes or flue with a low platform raised six or more inches above them. The sides and ends of a conservatory, up to the glass, should be built by boarding against the studs with matched flooring, the tongue side up, both inside and outside; by lining the outside with tarred building felt or boards against the studs, it will be warmer. After the wood work is finished it should receive several coats of paint, white being the color generally preferred.

Fig. 28.

Winter Management.—The conservatory in winter should be kept at as uniform a temperature in the night time—that is one night with another—as possible, and at a figure adapted to the requirements of the majority of the collection. I say *night* time, because the inside atmosphere is not then affected by influences of sun and clouds, which renders it easier thus to give and observe directions, besides in the day time a uniform temperature is undesirable, as plants in the conservatory require more heat when it is sunny than in cloudy weather. This should be carefully observed by inexperienced operators. A thermometer is indispensable to indicate the temperature. A temperature of 70° or even above, will suit any kind of plants, when the sun shines, provided air is admitted at the same time, while in cloudy days more than 10° above a suitable night temperature should be guarded against by checking the fire or admitting air. When airing, do not open the ventilators so much at once, as to greatly affect the temperature; a little air daily is desirable if the weather is not too severe. In warm spring, summer and autumn weather the ventilators may be kept wholly or partially open all the while. When the surface of the soil in pots indicates dryness, water should be freely applied with the watering pots, as plants are easily injured by becoming too dry. Looking over the collection every second day in winter, and daily in spring, watering where it is required, is none too often; in a house heated with the flue it is necessary to water daily over the hottest part. Water occasionally sprinkled over the plants renders the air humid, which is beneficial to all kinds of plant growths. The matter under head of a Classification of the Amateur's Work for Every Week in the Year, contains much other important information that has a bearing on conservatory management in winter as well as summer.

Summer Management.—If the glass roof be whitened *on the outside* with a thin wash made of quicklime and water, the home conservatory can be made a most delightful place all summer, otherwise the scorching rays of the summer sun would create a heat of sufficient intensity to nearly or quite cause the destruction of all plant life in the building; this wash should be applied about the first of June. With doors and ventilators open, by dashing water on the walks, and profusely sprinkling and watering the plants, etc., the atmosphere may be kept agreeable, and hanging baskets and all plants will thrive amazingly, particularly if abundant pot room has been afforded the latter. With the return of August and the two following months, the securing of plants from the open ground will require attention, and fire heat may be started a little in cool nights, but during the day, as late as possible in the season, the ventilators should be kept open. Always have a little sand on the benches where pots are set.

Propagation of all kinds of plants may be successfully done at any time in the conservatory. The bed in which the cuttings are struck should be boarded up on the sides, underneath, to cause the heat from the pipes or flue to rise up through the sand, for imparting the desired bottom heat to the bed. See special article on the subject of Propagation.

Insects, etc.—*Aphis or Green-fly* are very common intruders; these may be destroyed, and also prevented, by dampening one-fourth or one-half pound of dry refuse tobacco or stems from the cigar maker, and after placing it on a handful of shavings or live coals, on the ground or stone floor, burning to ashes. The smoke thus produced may be strong enough to be insupportable to human lungs and senses, without affecting plants. The presence of *Red Spider* indicates too dry an atmosphere, which should be corrected by dashing water about the house. Any plants affected by this insect should daily receive a thorough sprinkling or washing of water. *Mealy Bug* and *Scale* may be exterminated by washing and brushing the affected part of the plant. To remove *Angle Worms*, plants should be tapped out of the pots, and the worms picked from the ball of earth. Should mildew at any time put in an appearance, scatter a little flour of sulphur over the plants after the foliage is wet from watering.

COLD PITS FOR WINTER PROTECTION.—A cold pit, made by excavating the soil in some dry spot in the garden, to the depth of two feet and upwards, and of a size suitable to be covered with glass sash, forms one of the most inexpensive and efficient appliances that can be introduced into the flower garden. It will answer the purpose of wintering tender Roses, Carnations, and many other plants, much better than a cellar, especially if the latter is too dark, too damp or too warm; and, besides, provides a means of keeping up a succession of flowers of Alba Fimbriata and other Pinks, Roses, Deutzia, Iberis, Violets, Lily of the Valley, etc., during the winter in the house or conservatory, by carefully taking these up from the garden, and after potting, storing them in the cold pit, until they are brought into the heat and better light, which may be done at intervals during the winter and spring. Indeed, a conservatory can hardly be considered completely equipped without a cold pit near at hand to serve such a purpose. The sash used to cover the pit may be similar to those made for hot-beds, an ordinary size being six feet long, by three and one-half feet wide. The sides against the soil should be boarded up or walled up with brick or stone, which should run a foot above the surface at the rear, and nine inches above it on the front side, the top of the end walls having a regular slope from rear to front, and all finished to give support to the sash. Bank up the part of the wall that projects above the surface, and scatter an inch or two of coal ashes or gravel in the bottom of the pit, on which to place the plants. About all the attention such a pit requires after the plants are in, is to ventilate when the weather will allow, and to cover the glass with shutters or mats of straw or other material, sufficient to keep out hard frost in severe cold weather. Aside from one thorough watering when plants are potted, water should be sparingly given during winter.

Fig. 29. Climbing Rose—Gem of the Prairie.

THE ROSE FAMILY.

As a rule I think experienced cultivators are all ready to admit that Roses are easier to rear, in proportion to their value, than any other family of plants in cultivation; and yet there is scarcely a subject connected with floriculture, in which amateurs generally realize so great a lack of knowledge, as on the subject of Roses and their management. This can be accounted for by the fact that the family is extensive and greatly diversified, and consequently rather difficult to comprehend and become intimately acquainted with; but by carefully discriminating between the various classes into which the family is divided, bearing in mind the nature, adaptability and also treatment of each, there need be no more difficulty in becoming familiar with their culture, than with the cultivation of Lilacs and other hardy shrubs, Geraniums, or the tropical Coleus or Cannas, whose real, individual requirements, although simple and generally understood, are together quite as varied, as are the different classes of Roses, but as they do not belong to one natural family, and are known each by the distinct name it bears, their culture collectively appears more simple. Being desirous of rendering all possible aid in making Rose culture as popular as it deserves to be, I have treated the subject, with due regard to simplifying it, by treating upon the Hardy and Tender divisions of the family separately, and then describing the classes that are included in each, following up with directions for cultivating and managing the plants in summer and winter.

HARDY ROSES.

This division of Roses includes the classes *Hybrid Perpetual, June or Summer, Climbing, Moss, etc.*, and are all noted for their hardiness and easy culture.

HYBRID PERPETUAL ROSES.—This is by far the most desirable class of hardy Roses for general cultivation, being vigorous and robust in habit and producing flowers, usually very fragrant, that for immense size, perfect form and gorgeous and brilliant colors are unequaled. This class is of comparative recent introduction, having originated from hybridizing the June or Summer Rose with the ever-blooming section. Although the name would indicate the quality of blooming perpetually, only some varieties are strictly deserving of the term, as they flower freely but once in early summer, after which they can not be depended upon for more than a few flowers; but as an offset to such mis-application of the term "perpetual," the flowers of these varieties are likely to be possessed of more than ordinary perfect form, fragrance or color. The more prolific varieties, however, not only produce a wealth of flowers in June and July, but again at intervals during the summer, with usually an increase towards autumn. Although this class is comparatively hardy in this latitude, it is always best to protect with straw in winter. The remarks elsewhere relative to removing matured flowers apply with particular stress to Hybrid Perpetual Roses.

JUNE OR SUMMER ROSES.—The varieties of this class are all perfectly hardy, free growers, producing an abundant crop of flowers in June or early summer, and will thrive in any soil and under almost any circumstances. Specimens of this class are to be found in nearly every garden in the country. Many of the improved varieties are very desirable. The Hybrid China, Damask and Provence sections belong to this class.

HARDY CLIMBING ROSES.—This class, of which the Prairie Roses are the principal varieties, are adapted for covering walls, trellises, arbors, etc. They are well known for their perfect hardiness, rapid growth, fine foliage and beautiful and finely-shaped flowers, comprising many different colors. Gem of the Prairie, of which an illustration is given (Fig. 29), is noticeable as one of the best of this class.

MOSS ROSES.—An elegant and well known class of Roses, in most varieties producing large clusters of buds, entirely covered with a delicate, mossy growth which renders them the perfection of beauty while in a bud or half open state.

VARIETIES OF HARDY ROSES.—To distinguish the classes, the following abbreviations are used in the description of varieties: H. Perp., Hybrid Perpetual; Climb., Climbing.

Achille Gounad (H. Perp.), deep rose and crimson; full form, and large size.

Anna de Diesbach (H. Perp.), bright rosy carmine; a fine, large showy variety.

Augusta Mie (H. Perp.), clear waxy rose, large and finely cupped, very fragrant; an excellent Rose.

Baltimore Belle (Climb.), white with blush tint, very compact and double; of rapid growth; one of the best of the class ; excellent.

Baron Prevost (H. Perp.), bright rose shaded with crimson; large, free bloomer.

Beauty of Waltham (H. Perp.), bright rosy crimson, very large and fragrant, free bloomer; should be in every collection.

Blanch Vibert (H. Perp.), white.

Boursalt Elegans (Climb.), flowers purple crimson; a hardy rapid grower, with long flexible reddish shoots.

Cardinal Patrizzi (H. Perp.), brilliant dark crimson; very full and attractive.

Celine (June), cupped Rose, large and fine; a rapid grower, suitable for planting to pillars, etc.

Comte de Boubert (June), rosy red, of large size and free blooming habit.

Countess de Murinais (Moss), a pure white moss rose, large and double.

Couquette des Alpes (H. Perp.), shell-tinted white, of delicate appearance and beautiful color.

Claude Millon (H. Perp.), deep violet crimson; very desirable.

Crimson Moss (Moss), a beautiful mossy variety, of crimson color; free growing and attractive.

Double Margined Hep (June), a beautiful semi-double, nearly white, Rose, shaded with pink.

Dr. Faust (H. Perp.), light crimson; robust grower and free flowering.

Duc de Rohan (H. Perp.), bright crimson, large and double; beautiful.

Duplessis Morny (H. Perp.), bright purplish crimson; a good bloomer, particularly in autumn; free and healthy grower.

Eveque de Nimes (H. Perp;) deep bright crimson, large and fine form.

Francis I. (H. Perp.), deep rose color; a steady, rapid grower.

Gem of the Prairie (Climb.), light shade of crimson, large, perfectly double and of beautiful form; the flowers are borne on trusses numbering from ten to twenty buds on each; an excellent pot Rose if kept pruned to a bushy form; not perfectly hardy in the North, requiring to be protected. See engraving, Fig. 29.

Gen. Jacqueminot (H. Perp.), brilliant crimson scarlet, fragrant, very large and attractive, free grower and abundant bloomer; one of the best of this class. See engraving, Fig. 30.

Fig. 30. Hybrid Perpetual Rose—General Jacqueminot.

Gen. Washington (H. Perp.), brilliant, dazzling crimson, approaching vermillion, very large and
perfectly double, free and constant bloomer; should be in every collection.

George IV. (June), dark crimson, shaded with purple; attractive.

Grevillei, or Seven Sisters (Climb.), a remarkably vigorous grower, but rather too tender in our
climate to be reliable; flowers in clusters very profusely; color, several shades of rose.

Joasine Hanet (H. Perp.), reddish purple, blooming in clusters.

John Hopper (H. Perp.), deep rose, with crimson center, large and fine form; very beautiful.

Jules Margotten (H. Perp.), brilliant carmine, somewhat imbricated; a very fine Rose, being
large and attractive, fragrant, and a free bloomer.

King's Acre (H. Perp.), deep purplish rose, very large and double; strong grower.

La Reine (H. Perp.), beautiful clear bright rose; fine, full form, large and fragrant; a strong
grower.

Leon des Combats (H. Perp.), reddish scarlet; a beautiful, distinct and attractive Rose.

Leopold Hausburg (H. Perp.), brilliant carmine; very handsome.

Louis Odier (H. Perp.) crimson; globular in form and exceedingly regular; very fragrant.

Louis Napoleon (H. Perp.), rosy crimson; large, full and fragrant.

Madame Chas. Crapelet (H. Perp.), bright rosy crimson, large and vigorous; distinct.

Madame Chas. Wood (H. Perp.), brilliant crimson, shaded with purple, large and double; a
profuse bloomer and one of the finest sorts.

Madame de Trotter (H. Perp.), bright red, double and fine.

Madame Hardy (June), a double white Rose, large and full.

Madame Laffay (H. Perp.), beautiful clear flesh color, changing to transparent rose; very fine.

Madame Louise Carique (H. Perp.), bright rosy carmine, large and full; cupped.

Madame Plantier (Hybrid China), one of the finest hardy pure white Roses; large fragrant flowers, bloom in clusters very profusely; a variety well suited for cemetery planting.

Marquis de Boccella (II. Perp.), light flesh-colored rose, petals edged with crimson; very desirable.

Mrs. Reynolds (H. Perp.), clear cherry red and crimson, brilliant; good grower and free bloomer.

Pæonia (II. Perp.), rich transparent carmine, large, finely cupped and double; fine growing habit and every way desirable.

Pius IX. (II. Perp.), clear bright purplish rose, changing to rosy pink delicately shaded; large and desirable.

Prairie Queen (Climb.), deep pink, sometimes with a white stripe, compact and globular; a valuable Climbing Rose.

President Lincoln (H. Perp.), bright cherry crimson, large fragrant flowers; a strong grower and free bloomer; one of the best.

Princess Camile de Rohan (II. Perp.), rich velvety crimson, shaded to dark rose; large and fine.

Queen of the Belgians (Climb.), a white Rose of rapid slender growth.

Reine des Violettes (H. Perp.), deep violet red; double and of fine form. This is a seedling from Pius IX.

Scarlet Greville (Climb.), scarlet crimson.

Souv. de Henry Clay (H. Perp.), bright rosy pink; large and fine; vigorous grower.

Sydonia (II. Perp.), light pink; very large and full; one of our best fall-blooming Roses.

Triumph de l'Exposition (II. Perp.), bright reddish crimson, beautifully shaded.

Violet Blue (June), dark violet purple; very distinct.

William Griffeth (H. Perp.), rosy lilac, cupped and perfect form; vigorous and profuse.

William Jesse (II. Perp.), very dark velvety crimson; an attractive and distinct variety.

TENDER ROSES (MONTHLY).

In the division of Tender Roses we find characteristics that render the various classes of them, perhaps, the most desirable of all Roses for ordinary cultivation. They are natives of warm countries, like China, Bengal, the isle of Bourbon, etc., and although all the varieties will bear considerable freezing, and some are almost entirely hardy as far North as this latitude, their natural propensities to grow and flower, more or less, continually—monthly, as it is termed—remains unchanged with being removed to our climate, and with proper treatment and a suitable temperature in winter, in the window or conservatory, they may be had to flower the year through. In the mild climate of our Southern States they continue to grow and bloom in the open air with little interruption. By suitable protection at the approach of cold weather, or by wintering in a cold pit or cellar, they are easily managed to thrive in the open air in our Northern States, and produce an abundance of bloom from June until October and November.

BOURBON ROSES.—This is the hardiest class of this division of Roses, being nearly, but not quite, hardy in the latitude of Buffalo, and although some of the varieties do not flower as frequently as do those of other classes, the flowers are produced in large clusters, are of large size, well shaped, bright and varied in color, fragrant and lasting. Some, however, among which Hermosa stands prominent, are unequaled for their free flowering qualities, in the open air, and also for pot culture and winter flowering. All are vigorous growers, with rich luxuriant foliage, and are quite certain of giving satisfaction to the cultivator.

BENGAL OR CHINA ROSES.—The varieties of these Roses throughout are very free flowering, of thrifty growth and rather compact form, and while the flowers probably do not average as large as those of the Bourbon and other sections, the plants, if bedded out, are certain to be covered with a larger number of buds and flowers, of their characteristically brilliant colors, than any other class cultivated. Require protection during winter in the North. Very desirable for pot culture. The Agrippina is a well known and unequaled type of this class.

TEA-SCENTED ROSES.—Of the beautiful, sweet Tea-scented Roses it may be said, with mild justice to their many good qualities, that while the Rose finds devoted cultivators this class will rank highest among really fine kinds, in many respects; this, particularly, is true of the exquisite, deliciously fragrant, bud varieties, which, in the estimation of cultivated tastes, are, without exception, lovely and attractive above any flower in our collections, and they are nearly all remarkably suitable for pot cultivation, in the window or conservatory, as they are of fine habit and very productive. In our own experience in cultivating these in greenhouses (conservatories), where the varieties Safrano, Isabella Sprunt and Bon Silene are grown largely for our cut-flower trade, the plants never fail to produce a constant daily supply during winter and almost continually through the entire year. To show their appreciable value, I will state that these find ready purchasers all through cold weather, at the uniform price of fifteen cents per bud, just as cut from the plants, which is nearly twice the money realized for other Roses at the same time. True, the entire class are more susceptible of injury from cold than most Roses, nevertheless their general habit is healthy and vigorous, and when growing in the open ground they are amazingly prolific of buds and flowers, and by carefully lifting the plants in November, giving protection in a cold pit or cellar and returning to the open ground in spring, they will thrive from year to year the same as any other class of tender Roses. Some of the Tea-scented Roses are too double to be classified as bud-varieties—a few of which are not fully double when open. These produce large flowers of the unapproachable tints, shades and colors, and possesse.l of the tea-fragrance, for which this class is peculiar.

NOISETTE ROSES.—This class, although quite limited in number of varieties, is of great value for permanent planting in the soil of a greenhouse or conservatory, as by means of their free climbing habits they can be permanently trained to the rafters and trellises. Plants, after having spread to some distance, produce immense crops of beautiful, fragrant and fine colored flowers at intervals of quick succession. Severe pruning of the young shoots is necessary to secure the best results. By keeping the leading branches well cut back, numerous varieties of this class are excellent for growing as ordinary pot Roses and for bedding in summer.

VARIETIES OF TENDER ROSES.—To distinguish the classes, the following abbreviations are used in the description of varieties: Bour., Bourbon; Beng., Bengal or China; Tea, Tea-scented; Nois., Noisette. When the term *hardy* is employed, it is in a comparative sense:

Adam (Tea), pinkish purple color, of large size, but not blooming as freely as some.

Adrienne Christople (Tea), apricot yellow, shaded with rose; a beautiful variety.

Agrippina (Beng.), one of the brightest and most free-blooming Roses in cultivation and one that should be found in every collection; the flowers are of a deep crimson color, and double; excellent in the open ground or for pot culture.

Alice Walton (Beng.), rosy pink, very double and of fine form, flowers of small size; unrivalled as a hardy, free-flowering variety.

Appoline (Bour.), a fine large Rose, of robust growing habit, light pink, double and compact.

Arch Duke Charles (Beng.), rose, changing to deep crimson; good form and habit.

Beau Carmine (Beng.), light satiny crimson, double, medium to large size; fine compact grower.

Beauharnois (Beng.), a bright amaranth-colored Rose, quite distinct; of vigorous growth, and free-blooming habit.

Bella (Tea), perhaps the finest pure white Tea-scented Rose in existence when it is well grown. I find that the greatest difficulty with this recently introduced variety is, that being very double, it does not always open perfectly; vigorous and remarkably healthy.

Belle of Orleans (Nois.), this is a beautiful white Rose, and although small, it is perfectly double to the center; blooms with amazing freedom, in clusters, all through the season; a Noisette Rose, but well adapted to garden or pot culture, as its growth is easily controlled.

Bon Silene (Tea), very beautiful and desirable as a bud Rose; color purplish carmine with a peculiar bright rosy shade; rich, delicate tea-scented fragrance; good healthy grower.

Bouquet de Marie (Beng.), deep pink, of good form and habit.

Bourbon Queen (Bour.), rose color with salmon tint, large and double; a very fine variety.

Caroline de Manaise (Tea), white; a good bloomer and double; vigorous.

Cels (Beng.), blush; a very profuse bloomer, good and healthy grower; excellent.

Count de Ure (Bour.), salmon and carmine, quite double and fine; a very desirable Rose.

Count le Barthe (Tea), flesh color, changing to deep blush; very fragrant.

Compte Bobrinsky (Beng.), crimson scarlet, of good form.

Devoniensis (Tea), creamy white with rosy center; large and fine.

Duchess de Brabant (Tea), blush shade on rosy ground; unequaled for its delicate tint and satiny texture.

Fallemburg (Nois.), deep rose, fine form, and attractive.

Gen. Tartas (Tea), rosy pink of various shades; large, rather irregular, but very attractive; free bloomer, and healthy grower.

Gen. Wayne (Beng.), a medium sized deep crimson Rose of good substance, and a very free bloomer; sometimes the petals around the center are green.

Geo. Peabody (Beng.), light crimson, nearly white; free bloomer and a good compact grower

Gigantesque (Tea), flesh color, large size.

Glorie de Dijon (Tea), yellow shaded with salmon and rose; distinct and large.

Hermosa (Bour.), an old but very excellent Rose; clear rose color; double and very fragrant; a healthy, free-blooming variety. Should be in every collection.

Homer (Tea), rosy pink with salmon shade; fine form and a good bloomer.

Hymenee (Tea), a whitish rose with blush yellowish center.

Indica Alba (Beng.), pure white; small, free flowering.

Isabella Sprunt (Tea), a gem among Tea-scented Roses. Canary yellow; beautiful large buds, very sweet; profuse bloomer and free grower.

Joseph Gourdon (Bour.), a beautiful Rose; deep rose color; compact and double; very fragrant.

Julia Mansaise (Tea), pure white with slight yellowish tint; large and full; desirable in every collection; fragrant.

Lady Warrander (Tea), a beautiful white Rose, of fine habit and form.

Lamarque (Nois.), valuable white Rose; very double and fragrant; a luxuriant grower and very prolific; one of the best Roses in cultivation for conservatories.

Laurencia or Fairy Rose (Beng.), rosy pink; very small, of fine form and healthy growth.

Laurette (Tea), creamy white, shaded with rosy amber, very full and sweet; a free grower and excellent bloomer.

Fig. 31.   A Tea-Scented Rose-bud.   Fig. 32.   Hybrid Perpetual Rose in Pot.

Leveson Gower (Bour.), deep rose; large and full.

Louis Phillippe (Beng.), bright dark crimson; profuse bloomer; much like Agrippina.

Marechal Niel (Tea), the largest Tea-scented Rose in existence; perfectly double; finest pure chrome yellow, very fragrant; excellent for the conservatory and desirable for the garden; but requiring very careful culture when young; the buds are of immense size.

Madame Bravy (Tea), creamy white; large and fine.

Madame Breon (Beng.), rich rose changing to bright crimson, beautifully shaded; fragrant.

Madame Dumage (Tea), light rosy pink; a free-growing variety.

Madame Barrillet Deschamps (Tea), white, shaded with yellow; large and beautiful.

Madame Falcot (Tea), bright yellow shaded with crimson; a very attractive and desirable Rose.

Madame Jules Margotten (Tea), new; a very attractive Rose, with a novel intermixture of colors, ranging from canary yellow to apricot and violet.

Madame Russel (Tea), light pink shaded with a coppery hue; an excellent grower.

Madame de Vatry (Tea), deep rose shaded with dark crimson.

Malmaison (Bour.), a magnificent Rose; pale blush with fawn shade; large, double and full to the center; very fragrant; an excellent grower.

Marie Sisley (Tea), white, tipped and shaded with carmine.

Pactole (Tea), light canary shade; a good bloomer.

Pauline Labonte (Tea), bronzy yellow, large and sweet, very fine bud.

Paxton (Bour.), deep rose shaded with crimson; very strong grower, rich foliage and free bloomer.

Phœnix (Bour.), bright rosy purple; large flower; a good grower and free bloomer.

Pierre St. Cyr (Bour.), rosy crimson, large and full; very fragrant.

Premiere de Charissimer (Tea), a beautiful bud Rose; color bright purplish crimson.

President (Tea), rich light purplish crimson, with deep rose shading at base of petals; large and very attractive.

President d'Olbecque (Beng.), deep rosy crimson; free grower and bloomer.

Prince Eugene (Beng.), deep crimson; medium size.

Princess d'Esterhazii (Beng.), bright crimson with usually light stripes through the petals; double and very profuse; a fine garden Rose.

Pumilia (Tea), rich apricot tint, excellent either as a bud or an open Rose; dwarf, compact grower; free flowering and desirable.

Purple Crown (Beng.), rich purplish crimson, fine habit.

Roi des Cramoises (Beng.), deep crimson, very double and full, a dwarf compact grower, and profuse bloomer.   An excellent variety.

Safrano (Tea), a bud Rose of lovely color, which is somewhat difficult to describe, being a blending of rich apricot and saffron yellow colors; fragrant; free grower and abundant bloomer; one of the best Tea-scented Roses for pot or garden culture.

Sanguinea (Beng.), deep crimson; a profuse and showy variety for bedding; semi-double.

Solfaterre (Nois), a bright straw-colored Rose, free grower but well adapted for pot culture if kept pruned; a lovely, fragrant bud.

Triumphant (Beng.), deep crimson, medium sized, quite full and showy.
Triumph de Luxemberg (Beng.), brilliant crimson shaded with purple.
Washington (Nois.), white tinged with blush, blooms very freely in large clusters; vigorous.
White Tea (Tea), an old pure white Tea-scented Rose, still very desirable; free bloomer and
good grower.

CULTIVATION AND MANAGEMENT.

The Rosary.—Roses, to be most effective, should be planted in a bed by themselves,
where it is possible to do so. A dozen Roses scattered about the garden lose their individuality,
and are not nearly as attractive and interesting as when planted in a rosary of any shape the
grounds may allow or fancy suggest. Any fair garden soil that is well drained will answer
for them to grow in, although where a choice among different soils can be had, one of a loamy
clay nature would be found by cultivators preferable to any other, but whatever its character
may be, to attain anything like perfection in their culture it should be dug two spades deep,
and plenty of good stable manure thoroughly incorporated with it. During summer the surface
of the soil should be kept loose by cultivation. In planting the hardy varieties, including
Hybrid Perpetuals, which are to remain permanently in the beds, do not plant so close that they
will become crowded after attaining to some size; four feet is about right for this division,
although the tender varieties will do very well some nearer. Roses will not thrive in a situation
much shaded, and like all other fine plants they do better if not exposed to sweeping winds.

Pruning.—Usually the most pleasing shape to have Rose plants of, is a symmetrical,
bushy one, which can be produced by judicious pruning. With out-door Roses the proper
time to prune those that are entirely hardy is late in the fall, while the varieties that are liable
to be frozen back in winter should have the pruning deferred until early spring. All
strong shoots of the last season's growth should be cut back to two eyes, making the cut with
an upward slope directly above the upper eye, and weak growths should be entirely removed.
This will cause a vigorous growth of young wood, and will tend to increase the size and beauty
of the flowers. In pruning climbing Roses, only side shoots and such upright ones as may
appear superfluous, and all old wood that can be spared, should be cut away. The varieties of
the tender division, whose growth is almost continual, require pinching back of the strongest new
shoots during the season to keep them shapely, and all branches after they have budded and
flowered should be cut back sufficiently to induce a desirable number of new flowering shoots
to start into growth from the buds which are allowed to remain.

Insects injurious to Roses.—The most troublesome insect enemies of the hardy
Roses are the *Rose Saw-fly*, especially in its caterpillar state—then known as the *Rose Slug*—and
the *Rose Chafer or Bug*. As the depredations of each of these sometimes assume a serious form,
I will endeavor to describe them so that they may be known at their first appearance, and
that proper remedies may be applied in time for checking their ravages. During the last two
weeks of May, and until the middle of June, the *Rose Saw-flies* make their appearance upon the
plants, pair and lay their eggs in the incisions made with their saws in the leaves. They are of
a shiny black color, about one-fifth of an inch in length, and will be found mostly on the under
side of the leaves, or flying around from bush to bush. The first young slugs hatch out in a few
weeks after the flies appear, usually showing themselves about June 1st, and increasing in number during the month. These are of a pale green color and have an almost transparent, jelly-like
appearance. They feed upon the leaves, which soon look as if they had been burned, and drop
if the slugs are not destroyed. Dry slacked lime scattered over the leaves while wet with dew
is the most convenient remedy for destroying them, and will often prove effectual; but a more
destructive one may be had in frequently syringing the plant with whale oil soap dissolved
in water in the proportion of one pound to eight gallons of water; many of the female insects
in their beetle state—being more sluggish than the males—can be destroyed with this solution if
thoroughly applied by sprinkling or with a syringe every day as they first appear. No pains
should be spared to lessen the number as much as possible by this means. The *Rose Chafer*
is a small insect with a slender body, which tapers before and behind, measuring near three-
eighths of an inch in length, and entirely covered with ashen-yellow down. They usually appear
towards the middle of June, sometimes in large numbers, and remain from four to six weeks,
also feeding on some other plants besides the Rose. The usually efficacious remedies employed
in destroying other insects, scarcely effect these at all; and about the only way of destroying
them is to pass over the plants daily, shake or brush them into tin vessels containing water,
or they may be gathered on sheets and burned. *Red Spider* and *Green-fly* are the most common
insects met with in cultivating Roses in the window and conservatory, and directions are given
for preventing and destroying them, in the articles on "The Amateur's Conservatory," and
"Plant Culture in and about the House."

Mildew and Rust.—Mildew is a fungoid growth which shows itself upon the leaves
and small twigs of Roses and some other plants, both indoors and out. It has a gray mould-
like appearance, and seems to be invited by anything that causes the growth of the plant to be
suddenly checked. Roses, making a vigorous growth in the window or conservatory, if exposed
to a strong draft of cold air from the outside, will frequently be troubled with mildew, or by

allowing the soil to become dry enough to cause the leaves to droop will generally effect them similarly. All such unfavorable causes should be strictly guarded against. The ordinary agent, and undoubtedly the best, for eradicating and also preventing its appearance is flour of sulphur, which may be applied by dusting it upon the leaves after wetting down the foliage, every few days, until it is no more to be seen. *Rust* frequently troubles Roses in the garden, by appearing upon the leaves. The most efficient mode of preventing its spreading is to cut off and burn the infected branches, although if badly affected it may necessitate the sacrifice of the greater part of the plant.

Protection during Winter.

—Wherever it is possible, by means of protection, to keep Roses in the open ground during winter, I advocate the plan of so doing; but there will be little use of attempting to winter any but the most robust varieties, unless the ground is thoroughly drained, and when the rosary is in such condition, little loss need occur in leaving out many of the tender varieties in any part of the North, if suitable protection be provided. A most efficient method to adopt in protecting tender kinds, is to bend the plant to the ground, and completely cover with fine soil, from six to ten inches deep. In protecting Roses in a bed, the plants should all be bent in one direction, and the entire bed covered to the same depth. Another good way is to remove the top and bottom from a barrel or box, and placing it over the plant, fill loosely with leaves or straw. An amateur cultivator in Pennsylvania informs me that she succeeds in wintering tender Roses by laying them flat on the ground, and covering them with a board. Where the winters are very severe, and it is not considered desirable to risk tender kinds out of doors, they may be carefully taken up, pruned slightly, and placed in a cold pit until spring. By admitting an abundance of air in sunny spring days and warm weather they may be planted into the beds again by May 1st in this latitude. They should, however, be pruned again before planting out. Although most varieties of Hybrid Perpetual Roses will survive the coldest winters, unprotected, if growing on drained ground, it is a wise policy to cover them with straw late in autumn, being but little trouble, and they generally flower better with such treatment. A stake is firmly driven into the ground to each plant, and the plant tied nicely and rather close to it ; then some straightened straw is placed around the entire length of the plant—it need not be very thick—and the operation is completed by binding twine or straw bands around the whole, in several places. An application of stable manure or leaves around the base of the plant affords ample protection to the roots. All Roses, including the most tender kinds, will stand quite severe freezing without injury, and protecting the plants of any class should be deferred as late as possible in the fall. In spring, as soon as frost is out of the ground and growing weather at hand, all protection should be removed.

Roses for Pot Culture and Winter Blooming.

—The tender monthly Roses are nearly all suitable for pot culture and winter flowering, the Tea-scented section, with its unapproachable bud varieties, being usually preferred. Plants designed for winter blooming should be grown in pots during the previous summer. These should be plunged to the rim in earth or refuse hops, in order to prevent their drying out. Roses under any circumstances are quite susceptible of being injured by becoming too dry, and the condition should always be guarded against in pot culture. In the remarks on page 12, entitled "Preparatory Treatment of Plants designed for Winter Flowering," directions are given which apply to summer treatment of Roses grown in pots for this purpose. In August or September the plants should be repotted into larger sized pots, or planting into a box will answer quite as well. If they are to be grown in the window, they should now be gradually inured to the changed light and heat by keeping in the house part of each day only, and in the intervening time be given an airy exposure under the piazza or at the side of the house, lessening it by degrees as the season advances. If to be grown or "forced" in the conservatory, this means of acclimating is unnecessary, provided plenty of air is allowed to circulate through the structure after they have been taken in. Their winter position should be as much exposed to sun as possible, and the temperature kept at between 50° and 60° at night, with an increase of 15° higher during the day. Sprinkle the plants frequently, and never allow them to suffer from dryness of the soil.

Before dismissing this subject, I will explain how, by means of a cold pit, the Hybrid Perpetuals and many other hardy Roses, besides the entire division of tender Roses, may be taken up and made to do a kind of double duty, safely and with little trouble, by flowering profusely in the house or conservatory in March or later, and after being returned to the garden thrive there as usual. For this purpose any of the plants growing and flowering during summer are suitable without extra treatment. Dig them carefully late in October or November, in this latitude, and prune away the old straggling wood and superfluous shoots, cutting the remaining shoots back to several eyes; then pot into good fresh soil, one-third part of which should consist of well rotted manure, pressing it down quite firmly, and give a thorough watering when done. After this, place the potted Roses in the cold pit, where they are to remain until the middle of January and later for a succession. In bringing them in from the cold pit to the window or conservatory, do not place in too high a temperature at once. A situation indicating 40° or 45° will answer for them at first, and from this they may be changed to a temperature of from 50° to 60° at night, and receive treatment as directed for winter blooming plants. Contrary to what many persons might suppose, thus forcing Roses does not materially injure the usefulness of the plants, for by planting again into the garden in May, the monthly varieties will flower considerable, and all will regain their usual vigor during the summer.

DESCRIPTIONS OF IMPORTANT ORNAMENTAL

AND FLOWERING PLANTS, WITH CULTURAL DIRECTIONS.

The various families, species and varieties of plants which are desirable for cultivation on account of their flowering or other qualities, may be arranged according to their habits, means of reproduction, time and age at which they flower and mature, hardiness, etc., into a number of divisions and subdivisions, those commonly recognized being named and described herewith.

ANNUALS.

Plants that flower the first year from seed, and, after yielding a new crop of seed, die, root and all. Annuals are subdivided into two kinds—Hardy Annuals and Half-Hardy and Tender Annuals.

Hardy Annuals are those that germinate and make their growth to full maturity in the open air, without the aid of artifical heat, such as Sweet Pea, Nemophila, Mignonette, etc.

Half-Hardy and Tender Annuals differ from the Hardy Annuals in being more tender, on which account most of them should receive the assistance of artificial heat or protection during germination and in the early stages of their growth, although nearly all flower well later in the season if the seeds are sown in the open ground after all danger of frost to the young seedling is over. The Portulaca, Phlox Drummondii, Marigold, etc., belong to this division.

BIENNIALS

flower the second and sometimes the third year after sowing, then ripen their seed and die, root and all.

PERENNIALS

live and blossom from year to year, and, although some seed freely, as a rule they are shy in this respect, and are best increased by layers, cuttings, separation of the roots, etc. This division is subdivided into Hardy Herbaceous Perennials, and, in our latitude, Tender or Greenhouse Perennials, each of which include some Bulbous and Tuberous plants.

Hardy Herbaceous Perennials are understood to be plants, such as Pæonies, Hardy Phlox, Lychnis, Hyacinths, Lilies, etc., whose roots continue to live year after year, although the growth above ground dies annually, either soon after flowering or in the fall. Most kinds are propagated by division of the roots, which should be taken up for this purpose every few years, and then be reset. Some can also be increased from seed, others by layering.

Tender or Greenhouse Perennials for the most part consist of plants whose entire growth, both plant and root, is continual, and which are, with few exceptions, increased by slips or cuttings taken from growing plants. These plants are usually reared in pots, and belong to a division that, in some respects, is old and well-known, while in others it is still enveloped in clouds of ignorance and distrust relative to the kinds, in the minds of many amateurs. The well-known monthly Rose; Rose, Fish and Horseshoe Geraniums; the Lady's Ear-Drop; Snake and other Cactuses, Oleanders, Rosemary, etc., which all of us have been familiar with from infancy, almost, belong to this division, while many varieties and kinds, quite as easy of cultivation, and greatly improved, which have originated or been discovered within a score or a few years, are still comparatively unknown, and receive little attention, except from professional florists, and the more enthusiastic amateurs. It is to this class of plants that we are really indebted for many of our choicest floral gems, either for cultivating in the house, conservatory or garden. Sometimes plants belonging to the same botanical family vary so much that the family is properly arranged in several of the above divisions. This is the case with the Phlox family, some kinds of which are Hardy Annuals, and others Hardy Herbaceous Perennials; also with the flowering Pea and other families.

COMPARATIVE VALUE.—In this connection it may be well to consider the comparative value and prices of various kinds of plants, presuming that the reader, who purchases stock, desires to make the best possible investment with the money expended. Although prices of pot and other plants range higher than those of packets of flower seeds, it should be remembered that the former are always of considerable, often of a flowering, size when purchased, while plants still require to be reared from the latter; then, again, when once a plant is purchased it can be increased by cuttings, divisions, etc., to any desired extent, and the quality of the variety is never impaired, because the new propagation is *part* of the original plant with a root of its own. With seeds it is quite different; every experienced amateur knows that it is next to impossible to keep up a superior strain or variety of plants with seed, unless the seed is saved from plants grown isolated, after the manner practiced by professional seed-growers. The trouble is they are so apt to hybridize or mix, which necessitates the purchase of the same kind or variety each spring if it is considered desirable to keep up the stock; but even with this being necessary with varieties that cannot be saved sufficiently pure, the outlay to procure superior new seed need not be large each year, and it should be remembered that many of the cheap annuals and other seed-grown plants can be used with unequaled effect in producing display in the house or about the grounds.

In the descriptions of kinds which follows, the division to which each belongs is named in

3

the parenthesis preceding the regular matter. For an explanation of the figures and degrees which follow the names of Greenhouse Perennials, for instance ABUTILON (*Greenhouse Perennial, 33, 45, 85°*), see "Temperature," etc., page 20.

ABUTILON (*Greenhouse Perennial, 33, 45, 85°*).

This is a family of plants that are noted variously for their peculiar bell-shaped flowers of several beautiful colors, for the variegated character of the foliage of some varieties, and for the fine habits of others. All are adapted for house and conservatory culture in pots; some for bedding and others for planting vases and hanging baskets, and there is not a delicate or feeble growing variety among them. When bedded out in summer they can be taken up about September 1st and potted for winter decoration more readily than the average of plants. All should receive occasional pruning.

A. Mesopotamicum, calyx of the flower scarlet; petals yellow; of straggling, slender growth; excellent for training to a stake or trellis. *A. Mesopotamicum Pictum* a new variety, and one

Fig. 33. A Fine Double Balsam. See page 39.

of the finest drooping plants in existence for planting at the edge of baskets and vases, or for pot culture. The leaves are narrow, of beautiful shape and rather small, and are richly variegated with golden yellow on green, which renders the plant exceedingly valuable for contrasting with other drooping plants; as vigorous and healthy a grower as any. *A. Mesopotamicum variegata*, leaves are like Mesopotamicum, lance-shaped, but besides are variegated and marbled with clean yellow upon deep green in a pleasing manner; excellent slender habit. *A. Mesopotamicum striatum* (Fowering Maple), an upright grower of vigorous habit, producing its attractive drooping flowers nearly through the entire year. The flowers are about three inches in length, and orange, distinctly striped and netted with scarlet; foliage has the maple leaf shape, is clear and beautiful. *A. Thompsonii*, similar in most respects to the preceding variety, but the leaves are distinctly variegated, mottled and marbled with bright yellow on dark green ground. This variety is one of the best showy bedding and also pot plants for inside cultivation. It grows vigorously when planted out, and the distinctness of its leaf markings, although always striking, are greatly increased in beauty with the rapid growth it makes in summer. An excellent plant to set in vases, large hanging baskets, etc. *A. Santana*, purplish crimson flowers. *A. Santana alba*, an elegant upright growing variety, with pure white bell-shaped flowers. *A. Verschaffeltii*, a new variety, with deep green maple-shaped leaves, and exceedingly handsome lemon-yellow flowers; a stocky grower and profuse bloomer.

ACHILLEA (*Hardy Perennial*).

A family of hardy plants, mostly natives, several of which produce attractive flowers; they will thrive in any soil.

A. Ageratum has golden yellow flowers. *A. Millefolium* is a pretty rose-colored variety. *A. Ptarmica fl. pl.*, a double pure white variety, which is desirable in every collection. It continues to bloom most of the season, throwing up a succession of its pretty double flowers, in corymbs, on stems about one foot high. The foliage is dark shining green; very hardy.

ACHRYANTHES *(Greenhouse Perennial, 35, 50, 90°).*

A class of beautiful foliage plants most of which are excellent for planting in masses and in the ribbon style, their distinct colors forming a striking contrast with Centaureas and other white foliaged plants. All are admirably adapted for planting in the center of hanging baskets and vases, and are also suitable for house and window culture, as they develop their best colors even in partial shade and prove to be somewhat hardier than Coleus for this purpose. One to one and a half feet high. Any of the varieties strike root readily from cuttings, and all that is necessary to have beautiful medium-sized plants for window culture in winter or to plant in ferneries—for which purpose they are admirably adapted—is to propagate in July or August.

A. Aureus reticulatus, leaves are light green, netted with golden yellow, occasionally splashed with crimson; stalk and leaf-stems light crimson: altogether a beautiful and desirable plant. *A. Gilsonii,* leaves striped with various shades of carmine; stems of a deep shade of pink; in some respects an improvement on old Verschaffeltii, being of a more dense and compact growth; excellent in every way. *A. Lindenii,* an upright dwarf grower, about one foot high, completely branched from the root; leaves narrow lanceolate, of a deep, blood-red color, reflecting varying tints of red and purple; unsurpassed for bedding. *A. Lindenii aureus variegata,* a new variety, in every respect similar to Aureus Reticulatus, except that it resembles Lindenii in growth and form of leaf.

ACROCLINIUM *(Half-hardy Annual).*

This is one of the several useful everlasting flowers most readily grown from seed. The flowers are of medium size, good form, and are not excelled by any other kind in points of delicacy and beautiful tints. It is better to start the young plants in heat and transplant to eight inches apart, then to sow directly where they are to bloom, although there is no great danger of failure by doing so about June 1st, especially as the flowers should be cut for use in winter before they are fully expanded.

A. Album, pure white. *A. Roseum,* bright rose.

AGAVE—CENTURY PLANT *(Greenhouse Perennial, 32, 45, 90°).*

This remarkable and beautiful family of plants belongs to the class known as *fleshy* plants, which consist of those growths that have thick leaves and that present but a small amount of surface in proportion to their bulk. In the present instance the plant has no proper stem previous to the time it sends up its flowering shoot, which, as is well known, takes place at an advanced age, although the popular impression that they never flower until the age of one hundred years has been attained is erroneous. In Central and South America, their native habitats, they flower previous to their twentieth year, but in our greenhouses not usually until they have reached three or four times this age. After flowering, the plant dies to the ground, but the root continuing to live sends up new shoots. The leaves are long, thick and terminate in a point; they diverge upwards and outwards from the center and altogether contribute to form one of the most effective single specimen pot plants for decorating the grounds in summer and the conservatory or dwelling in winter that can be cultivated. The Agaves are easy to grow, being not at all particular as regards light or heat, in this respect being similar to the varieties of the Cactus family, and quite as desirable for house culture. Their growth can be retarded or encouraged by more or less frequently shifting them into larger pots, which, at the most, should not be done oftener than once a year.

There are two varieties in ordinary cultivation—*A. Americana,* with bluish-green leaves, and *A. Americana variegata,* similar in appearance to the preceding, except that the foliage is striped its entire length.

AGERATUM *(Greenhouse Perennial, 33, 45, 75°).*

The Ageratums are rapid growing, profuse blooming, easily propagated plants, that will thrive with the most ordinary treatment, either if bedded out or in pots, and are deserving of a place in every collection. The flowers are produced in compact tuft-like heads, and although no striking colors or any great variety of shades exist, in the different sorts, they appear in large numbers continually throughout the summer; are of excellent form and have long convenient stems for bouquet making, which render them important flowers for working into summer bouquets. On account of their being continually in flower, most of the varieties are valuable for planting in ribbon lines or for massing, and as they are easily reared from cuttings this fact should not be overlooked. One variety has handsome variegated foliage that creates a very pretty effect when similarly employed. Ageratums can be forced into flower in winter, either in the dwelling or conservatory, but are not prominently valuable for this purpose, although young summer propagated plants can readily be kept in a growing condition from which to take cuttings for spring stock.

A. Imperial Dwarf, is of compact low growth, attaining the height of eight inches, and spreading to the size of one foot across; it is almost entirely covered with porcelain-blue flowers during the greater part of summer. *A. Mexicanum* is one of the best for cut flowers; the flowers are of a delicate lavender blue color, and very freely produced; the plants grow to a height of from eighteen to twenty-four inches. *A. Mexicanum variegatum,* a beautiful variety of similar height to the preceding, the leaves of which are variegated with yellow, green and generally a faint shade of crimson; suitable for bedding or for pot culture. *A. Prince Alfred*, of dwarf habit, having flowers of a delicate lilac shade. *A. Tom Thumb*, the smallest variety of all, rarely attaining more than six inches in height; flowers of a light porcelain blue color.

AGROSTEMMA *(Hardy Annual)*.

A family of plants that flower freely in summer, and although not as valuable as many kinds, they may be grown with the greatest ease from seed, and having long stems and rather attractive colors and forms, are pretty in bouquets and other floral arrangements.

The varieties commonly grown are *New Scarlet*, a bright colored variety, *Cæli Rosa*, of a deep rose color.

ALOYSIA CITRIODORA—LEMON VERBENA *(Greenhouse Perennial, 33, 45, 80°).*

A neat growing shrub, with elegant light green lanceolate leaves that are undoubtedly more deliciously fragrant than those of any other plant in cultivation. It is a difficult matter to describe a fragrance with words that may be rightly comprehended. The fragrance of this plant somewhat resembles that of lemon fruit, yet besides possesses a pure sweetness and wholesomeness that is indescribable. I occasionally meet with persons of cultivated tastes, to whom the fragrance of such flowers as the Heliotrope, Mignonette, Tuberose, Jasminum, etc., which are prized by nearly every one, are found to be surprisingly distasteful, but I have yet to find the person to whom the fragrance of the Lemon Verbena is not agreeable in the highest degree. Although the Aloysia is a tender perennial, it sheds its leaves in the fall, and enters into a natural state of rest during winter, in which condition it is kept over until spring in some moderately dry place, like under the shelving in a conservatory or on a shelf in the cellar away from frost. The soil about the root should not be allowed to become dust dry, but at long intervals may be treated to a small quantity of water. In March or April it should be brought to light and be watered frequently to induce a new growth for the season. It may also be pruned at this time. The plant is suitable either as a pot plant or for bedding out, and will prove itself to be one of the easiest to cultivate.

ALTERNANTHERA *(Greenhouse Perennial, 35, 60, 90°).*

A genus of ornamental foliage plants, with variously marked leaves, that are well adapted for pot culture, baskets, vases, and for bedding out in ribbon lines or edging to flower beds, being of similar sizes and contrasting beautifully with variegated Alyssum and Thyme for such purposes. They grow rapidly, and form compact, globular-shaped plants of from five to twelve inches high, which are extremely beautiful. In hot August weather young plants can readily be obtained from cuttings for winter decoration and from which to propagate spring stock. The plants are quite easily injured by frost and should be planted out late enough in the spring to avoid danger from this cause.

A. Amabilis, the foliage of this variety is finely variegated with orange, rose and green; vigorous. *A. Latifolia*, broad smooth leaves, with many bright colors and tints on green ground resembling autumn leaves. *A. Spathulata*, leaves carmine and green, the carmine predominating; five inches. *A. Spectabile*, leaves orange, bronze and scarlet. *A. Versicolor*, a beautiful and distinct variety of rose and deep crimson color; nine inches.

ALYSSUM, SWEET *(Hardy Annual)*.

A pretty little plant, easy to rear from seed and to cultivate in summer and winter for bouquets, its pure white scented flowers, which are produced abundantly, rendering it valuable for this purpose. For summer culture sow in the open ground where it is to bloom, or transplant from the seed bed; in either case leaving four inches of open space between the plants. It is also a useful plant for hanging basket and vase culture. To have an abundance of flowers in winter, sow about July 1st and cultivate in pots during summer. This plant is perennial in habit if the flowers are picked and it is kept in a growing temperature.

ALYSSUM, VARIEGATED SWEET *(Greenhouse Perennial, 35, 50, 80°).*—This is a pretty variegated variety that is grown from cuttings. It is quite similar in appearance to the above variety, but white predominates over the green in the leaves, making it exceedingly ornamental, aside of its many white sweet scented flowers; although one of the finest droopers for planting at the edge of hanging baskets and vases, and also as a pot plant, it is one of the very best low bedding plants for planting in ribbon lines or for edgings, as it assumes a dense compact form when bedded.

AMARANTHUS *(Half-Hardy Annual)*.

While some varieties of the Amaranthus family are highly esteemed as garden and pot plants for their beautiful, showy foliage, and others for the fantastic form and arrangement of the flowers and foliage, some usually advertised in seedmen's catalogues are scarcely deserving of culture, unless planted in the back ground, or grouped with plants to be seen from a distance, on account of the coarseness of the foliage and flowers, but these are so easily grown from seed, which may be sown directly where they are wanted, that after all perhaps they are entitled to our consideration. As a rule, both the flowers and foliage of the various Amaranthus are more brilliant in a poor soil and also in dry seasons.

A. Bicolor Ruber, a very fine, new bedding plant, the seed of which should be sown in heat in March or April; the lower half of the leaf a red scarlet, the upper half maroon, sometimes

Fig. 34. Begonia Weltoniensis.

tipped with yellow. The plants are not always true to color, especially when grown on rich soil. *A. Caudatus* (Love Lies Bleeding), red, graceful; 3 feet. *A. Cruentus* (Prince's Feather), crimson; 3 feet. *A. Melancholicus Ruber*, a very showy plant of fine growth, foliage blood-red; well adapted for ribbon belts or groups; one and one-half feet high. *A. Salicifolius*, the Fountain Plant, from the graceful manner in which the foliage is arranged; the leaves are elon-gated and willow-shaped, and of a bronzy carmine hue; sow the seed in heat. *A. Tricolor* (Joseph's Coat), leaves red, yellow and green; very handsome in a favorable season.

AMARYLLIS FORMOSISSIMA, JACOBEAN LILY *(Tender Bulb).*

There are several species of the Amaryllis family, all of which produce flowers of marvel-ous beauty, but the variety named at the head of this matter is one of the most common as well as one of great beauty. The flowers are large, of a drooping lily-like shape, and of the most brilliant dark crimson color; they are produced on a stalk a foot high; in the sunshine they have the appearance of being sprinkled with gold. The bulb may be planted out the latter part of May, in rich sandy soil, to a depth at which the neck of the bulb shall be even with the soil; it will flower in June or July. After the tops have been cut down by frost in Septem-ber or October, the bulbs should be lifted and put away in dry sawdust, safe from frost. The Amaryllis is well adapted to pot culture in the conservatory or on the window-shelf; give an abundance of water until after flowering, when it should be gradually and finally altogether withdrawn. After several months of rest it may be repotted for another season of flowering.

AMOBIUM ALATUM *(Hardy Annual).*

A pretty little everlasting flower of fine appearance, which ranks very high for winter bou-quets, on account of its unequaled pure white color, if they are gathered and cured by hanging in the shade before being fully expanded; also useful for cutting fresh. Grows freely in any garden soil.

ANEMONE *(Hardy Tuber)*.

Although generally known as a hardy tuberous plant, the Anemone Hortensis is not sufficiently so to render it safe to plant them out in the open ground in the fall along with Hyacinths and the other hardy bulbs. By keeping them out of the ground and at the earliest opportunity in the spring planting them in a bed prepared the fall previous, and that has been kept covered, they will succeed very well, and will flower from April until July. The flowers are produced on erect stems, six to nine inches in height, in both double and single varieties; they are of the most brilliant colors with beautiful marks and stripes. Plant the tubers, which have a curious appearance, resembling ginger roots, about six inches apart and three inches deep. After they have produced their flowers for the season, and the leaves turn yellow, the roots may be taken up, dried in the shade and put away for planting again.

ANEMONE JAPONICA *(Hardy Perennial)*.—This is a very desirable hardy plant, introduced from Japan. There are several varieties—*A. Rubra*, with red flowers, and *A. Alba* white, being the most commonly cultivated. The flowers of these are almost two inches in diameter, and are produced in great profusion for a long time the latter part of summer and in autumn; the plants attain a height of two feet. There are different varieties of wild or wood Anemones found growing in various portions of the United States and Europe, which are very attractive among other early wild flowers.

ANIMATED OATS *(Hardy Annual)*.

Among those vegetable growths which partake of a curious character, the seed of this plant is prominent and interesting. Of itself it has a strong resemblance to an insect with long cricket-like legs, and being bearded and covered with spurs, all pointing in one direction, it will throw itself ahead with a darting, springing motion sufficiently life-like in appearance to be deceptive if laid upon a paper which is being agitated; or if the seeds are moistened, so sensitive are their strong beards to alternations of dryness and moisture, that they will twist and keep the seed in motion, resembling an insect crawling on the ground. Sow in the open ground.

ANTIRRHINUM—SNAP-DRAGON *(Hardy Herbaceous Perennial)*.

I class the Antirrhinum among hardy perennials because it is of perennial habit, and will survive our winters with protection, although it is not to be entirely relied upon in this respect, as some seasons it will die out. It is, however, grown so readily from seed, sown either in the latter part of summer or early in the spring, in the frame or hot-bed or in the open ground, that there is no necessity of keeping up the old plants. Flowers freely the first season from the seed, and better the second, if the flowers are removed as fast as they appear the first season. The flowers are bright and attractive, appearing for a long time and until cold weather; also easily propagated by cuttings, and stock plants can be kept over in a cold-pit until February or March, and then started into growth to form shoots for this purpose. Among the Antirrhinums are the tall (two feet high), dwarf (one foot high) and Tom Thumb (six inches high) sections, the following being some of the most distinct varieties:

A. Album, pure white, both tall and dwarf. *A. Brilliant*, crimson and white, both tall and dwarf. *A. Delila*, carmine, white throat. *A. Firefly*, orange scarlet, white throat, both tall and dwarf. *A. Papillon*, scarlet, white and yellow, both tall and dwarf. *A. Purpureum*, deep bright purple; dwarf. *A. Striatum*, beautifully striped; tall, dwarf and Tom Thumb.

AQUILEGIA—COLUMBINE *(Hardy Herbaceous Perennial)*.

A family of plants that flower the first part of the season, some varieties of which are well known, the old garden Honeysuckle being one of these. They may be propagated by dividing the roots, or some of the varieties by seed.

A. Cœrulea, a beautiful variety recently introduced from the Rocky mountains, and which is entitled to be generally cultivated. In England I see it is declared to be "not only the Queen of Columbines, but even the most beautiful of all hardy herbaceous plants." The color is a delicate blue, with distinct white center, and the remarkably long spurs give the flower an appearance both singular and striking.

ASTER *(Hardy Annual)*.

The Aster is one of the grandest families of seed-grown plants that can be cultivated. There are tall growing varieties two to three feet in height, and from these, different varieties range variously in height, all the way down to the very dwarf, not more than eight inches high, and which spreads out so as to present the appearance of a bouquet of flowers set in the ground. The flowers are of the most attractive, as well as delicate, colors, including pure white, and present quite a variety of forms, many of them being very large and double to the center. The seed may be started early in the hot-bed, cold-frame, or seed-bed, as the young plants transplant readily, or it may be sown in the open ground directly where they are to flower. Transplant the large varieties to about ten inches apart, and the dwarf from that down to six. The tall varieties should be supported by stakes in summer to prevent the rain from bending or breaking them down.

A. Bouquet, Newest Dwarf, a very fine acquisition, each plant looks like a bouquet of flowers; eight inches. *A. Bouquet, Dwarf Pyramidal*, ten inches high, and an early and abundant bloomer. *A. Chrysanthemum-flowered, Dwarf Double*, a splendid variety of dwarf compact habit, nine inches in height, producing flowers three to four inches across. *A. Cocardeau, or New Crown*, a fine flower; very double; the central petals being pure white, sometimes small and quilled; sports occasionally; eighteen inches. *A. German, Pyramidal-flowered*, late, branching, good habit; needs no tying. *A. German, Quilled*, desirable on account of the quilled appearance of the flowers; about three feet high. *A. Hedge Hog, or Needle*, petals long, quilled and sharply pointed, very curious and fine; two feet. *A. La Superbe*, large flowering class, often more than four inches in diameter, twenty inches in height. *A. Pæony-flowered perfection, Truffaut's Newest*, one of the best; very large, beautiful flowers; petals long and a little reflexed; two feet. *A. Pearl*, this is entitled to be called a gem among Asters; is of dwarf, compact, bushy habit, not above fifteen inches in height, closely set with beautiful imbricated, double, globular flowers of good colors. *A. Rose, Improved*, a valuable class of Asters, producing very double and large flowers. The blood-red color of this variety is the darkest and most brilliant of all Asters; two feet. *A. Victoria*, flowers very double, imbricated, globular and large; the plant is very robust, about two feet in height and branching. *A. Victoria, Dwarf*, only one foot in height, but very rich flowering, with flowers three to four inches across. *A. Emperor, Giant*, very brilliant and beautiful colors, flowers double and of immense size, often four inches in diameter; two feet.

ASTILBE JAPONICA—Spirea Japonica *(Hardy Herbaceous Perennial).*

One of the most beautiful of all hardy plants. It blooms the forepart of summer, in upright spikes of pure white, delicately-formed flowers; the foliage is of compound digitate form, and exceedingly attractive, being also of a deep, uniform green color; height of plant, one and a half to two feet. By potting the Astilbe at the approach of winter, it may be taken into the dwelling or conservatory, and forced into bloom, by which means it becomes very attractive, and thrives readily.

AZALEA *(Greenhouse Shrubby Perennial, 32, 50, 70°).*

Plants of high value for window and conservatory decoration, being covered with one blaze of beauty in the spring months, and continuing to increase in splendor and the profusion of flowers with each year's growth. In summer they may be moved to the open air, and the pots plunged to the rims in soil in some shady place, such as against a fence or building, until September, when they should be taken, for the winter, either into the conservatory direct, or cellar or cold-pit, to bring in for flowering at any time between February and May. The most suitable time for re-potting is after their flowering season; they delight in a light soil containing some loam from the woods.

BALSAM—Lady's Slipper *(Tender Annual).* See Fig. 33.

Balsams are a class of plants readily grown from seed, that bountifully repay any time and expense involved in rearing them. Their double flowers, of most brilliant colors and shape, with the beautiful texture of the petals, rank them among the finest of flowers, but unfortunately being short stemmed, their use in ordinary bouquets is precluded; they can, however, be employed in arranging plate bouquets or upon baskets of moss, very well. The pure white variety is largely grown by florists for making into wreaths, harps and other designs, suitable for funerals, by first stemming them with wire on short bits of match stick and inserting into wire forms filled with moss, so that the flower touches; frequently no other flowers are used but the double white Balsam, and the effect produced is complete. For ordinary culture the seed may be sown in the hot-bed, cold-frame, or seed-bed, transplanting the plants finally, to a distance of ten or twelve inches apart, after the second set of leaves have started. Few plants are susceptible of such great improvement by pinching as is the Balsam; they may be trained to one, three or five branches for flowering, and in either case will be more pleasing than if allowed to take their natural course in growing, or some plants may be trained to each method, thus creating a variety in themselves. To train to one branch, simply remove all side shoots as they appear; this will cause it to grow two or three feet in height, and be perfectly covered with bloom. For three or five shoots, pinch back the terminal and all side shoots but the number it is desired to have remain for flowering. The American climate is well adapted to the Balsam, and if grown in good rich soil, flowers of great excellence can be produced, although it seems to be an established fact that some flowers will come only partially double from the best strains of double seed. The plant is well adapted for pot culture in summer, by having the soil of good loamy quality, well enriched, and giving it a sunny position and plenty of water. Nothing smaller than a six-inch pot will answer well for this purpose.

B. Camellia-flowered, spotted German, very double and choice, spotted with white. *B. Camellia-flowered*, pure white. *B. Camellia-flowered, double dwarf*, very fine; eight or ten inches in height. *B. Carnation*, fine double flowers, resembling a Carnation. *B. Victoria*, satiny white, spotted with scarlet; exceedingly pretty. *B. Rose-flowered*, perfectly double. *B. Extra Double Dwarf*, very double; eight inches.

BEGONIA *(Greenhouse Perennial, 36, 55, 80°).*

An interesting family of plants in their two divisions of flowering and showy leaf varieties. The more free-flowering varieties of the former are indispensable in every florist establishment, their flowering qualities rendering them valuable for bouquets. They are also well adapted for

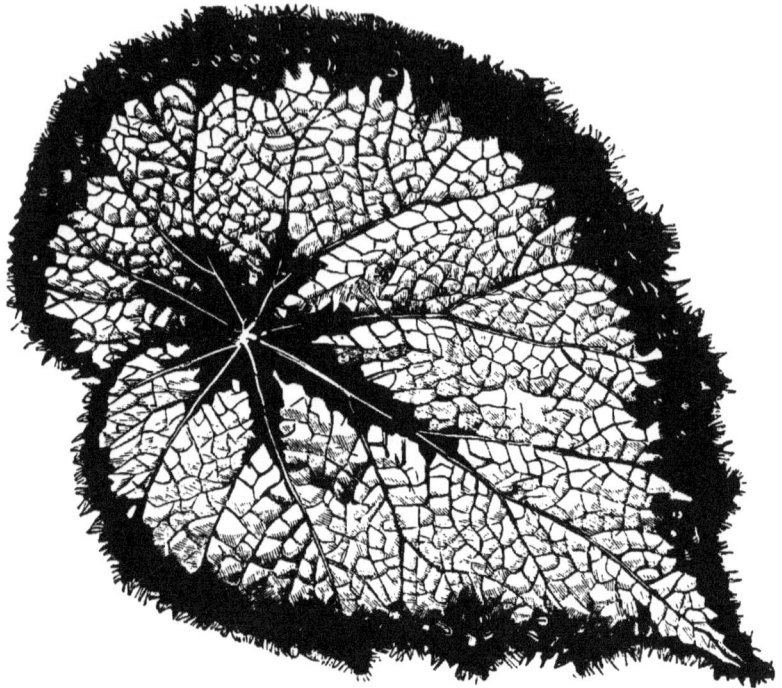

Fig. 35. Begonia Rex.

pot culture in the window, or out-of-door plant stand, and in hanging baskets, and also Fern-eries, but possess no real value for bedding in the garden unless planted in a warm place well protected from winds. During the greater portion of the year the plants are covered with a profusion of gracefully drooping racemes of rose, pink, white and crimson buds and blossoms of an exceedingly attractive, waxy, coral-like appearance. The plants are of neat, compact habit, with glossy green leaves in some varieties and exquisitely cut, in others. Both sections of the Begonia family delight in warm, sandy, well-enriched soil.

B. Fuchsioides coccinea, deep scarlet; quite a free grower, although all are good in this respect. *B. Glaucaphyllia scandens,* an early flowering variety, producing its clusters of rich salmon-colored flowers from the axle of each leaf; the plant being of a lovely drooping habit, it is exceedingly fine for hanging baskets, in a warm place. *B. Hybrida multiflora,* a remarka-bly neat and free-flowering variety, with small, ovate, glossy leaves, and many rosy pink blos-soms; excellent. *B. Nitida,* a strong growing variety, producing beautiful, large, salmon-colored flowers. *B. Nitida alba,* a free growing, profuse-blooming variety, producing panicles of pure white flowers during the winter months. *B. Palmata,* attractive, palm-shaped leaves *B. Parviflora,* dwarf; a neat growing plant, with white flowers; blooms most profusely in summer, when its flowers are useful for bouquets. *B. Saundersonii* (Coral Begonia), one of the best flowering Begonias; the flowers are of a scarlet shade of crimson, borne in profusion during the entire winter months; leaves slightly edged with scarlet. *B. Weltoniensis,* this valuable acquisition, of recent introduction, I consider deserving of more than an ordinary notice. It is a rapid, healthy grower, very profuse bloomer, with beautiful foliage, and always presents an attractive appearance, summer and winter. Fig. 34 represents a pot plant of this variety, and also the individual leaf and flowers, but it is impossible to fairly portray them in the black and white of a wood engraving. The richness of the surface of the leaves, in a natural specimen, show various shades of dark and light green colors of intense richness, and presents a transparent depth of texture, without any gloss whatever, of the most exquisite beauty, being somewhat similar—except in color—to the bloom on the grape. The flowers and buds are a beautiful pink color, and are produced in clusters, by the hundred, on an ordinary sized plant, with common culture. The leaf-stalk and the entire stalk and branches of the plant are dark crimson, and sufficiently striking to create a contrast, which is as remarkable as it is rare, among plants, with the brilliant green leaves and the pink flowers. Unlike many plants that possess unusually meritorious characteristics this new Begonia is unexcelled by any of the old tested varieties, for freeness of growth and flowering qualities, and the plant naturally assumes a well-proportioned form.

SHOWY-LEAF BEGONIAS.—Of the show leaf varieties I will state that lovers of the beautiful in Nature's grotesque growths will find in this entire division much to admire. Their large, attractive and interesting leaves, add an effect to collections of plants which can be equaled by nothing else grown. Fig. 35 represents a leaf of the Rex variety, at about one-fourth the natural size of well grown leaves. Imagine in the engraving the light part of the leaf to be a bright greenish silver hue; the center and outer edge a lively, almost black green in some places, or rather several shades of green, spotted lightly with silver. Imagine the upper surface of the leaf-ribs to be studded with small crimson hairs, while the extreme edge is fringe-like, with a crimson scarlet color, as is also the underside, and with this the veins distinctly prominent and showy, and you can form an idea of the beauty of this entire section. All the varieties are suitable for pot culture, and for hanging baskets in protected places. They delight in a warm, shady, place, and should not be exposed to sweeping drafts of air. In habit and general appearance the first and last named varieties in the following descriptions are quite similar to the flowering section, being upright growers, with branches, while the others are prostrate in habit, although the leaves stand well up on strong stems.

B. Argyrostygma Veitchii, a very handsome variety, leaves smooth, of medium size, light green and thickly covered with small, clear silver markings; underside, of a crimson color, smooth; white flowers; easy to cultivate. *B. El Dorado*, medium sized leaf, distinctly marked and of a peculiar velvety texture. *B. Insignis*, a free grower, leaves of medium size with a metallic lustre. *B. Luxuriance*, leaves nearly star-shaped, borne on stems a foot long; grotesque. *B. Mary Stuart*, large showy leaves; an old favorite, perhaps the best in cultivation. *B. Mrs. Victor Lemoine*, light colored leaf, with the edges and center beautifully marked like lace. *B. Queen of Begonias*, a good grower. *B. Rex*, a fine variety; excellent, described above. (See Fig. 35). *B. Silver Queen*, a variety in which the silvery color predominates. *B. Zebrina*, a beautiful upright grower of bold appearance, with thick leathery leaves from four to six inches long and two wide in their widest parts; of a very dark green color, striped with silvery marks; underside and stems of dark crimson and red colors; a very handsome variety.

BOUVARDIA *(Greenhouse Perennial, 35, 60, 90°).*

A highly useful family of shrubby plants for the greenhouse and the window, if warm and sunny, and for bedding out, blooming all summer in the beds, and when properly prepared in pots will also bloom continually during winter in the conservatory or other suitable place. Thousands of feet of glass are each year devoted to the culture of Bouvardias alone, for bouquet flowers in the vicinity of our large cities. The flowers are of an exceedingly beautiful, substantial, waxy character, of bright and desirable colors, from the purest white to scarlet. A mellow open soil is best suited for the Bouvardia. As it requires a high temperature for its growth, the plants should not be bedded out in the latitude of Buffalo before the latter part of May. For winter flowering they should be started the spring previous, and grown in about five-inch pots until September, when they may be shifted into a larger size for flowering (observe directions for summer and fall treatment on page 14). Towards spring the flowering and other shoots should be severely pruned back to induce a stocky new growth for summer flowering. With one exception, Bouvardias are only propagated by root cuttings and by a course of treatment hardly practical outside of a good propagating house.

B. Davidsonii, a free flowering, pure white variety; excellent and distinct. *B. Elegans*, vermillion red, bright and free blooming; the most generally cultivated of all. *B. Hogarth*, dark crimson. *B. Jasminoides*, pure white; susceptible of being increased from cuttings. *B. Leiantha*, scarlet, profuse; one of the best.

BROWALIA *(Half-Hardy Annual).*

A class of flowers usually grown in the garden, but also quite suitable for pot culture. There are two varieties, the colors of which are blue and white respectively. The flowers are not large, but are pretty and distinct, and are freely produced for a long time on a stalk a foot and a half high. The seed may be sown in the open ground where they are to flower, or in a protected bed, from which they may be transplanted to a distance of twelve inches apart.

BUTTERCUP. See Ranunculus.

CACALIA—FLORA'S PAINT BRUSH *(Half-Hardy Annual).*

Plants grown with the greatest ease from seed, which may be sown in the open ground in May, or earlier in the hot-bed, or other protected situation, and afterwards transplant them to the garden. The flowers range from scarlet to yellow in color, are bright and pretty, and somewhat resemble a miniature brush; they are small and produced in clusters on long stems, on which account they are useful for bouquets, although not strikingly brilliant. The plants attain a height of from eighteen inches to two feet, and are in bloom throughout the summer months.

CACTUS *(Greenhouse Perennial, 35, 50, 95°).*

A well known family of succulent, fleshy plants, all of which are natives of the warmer regions of America. They are desirable as pot plants, on account of the remarkably singular forms of growths which the various species assume; their almost unexceptional beautiful flowers which are produced in ordinary culture, and the ease with which they are cultivated, either in the window or conservatory. To grow the Cactus readily all that is necessary is to imitate the natural conditions of their growth. They are found in their greatest perfection in sections which are subject to severe drouths of long duration, alternate with long wet spells, and accordingly a free application of water should be given for three or four months and then be withheld almost wholly during the rest of the year. They may be kept dryest during winter, but not in a place where it is cold. Repotting them frequently is not agreeable with their well doing, and it should be done not oftener than once a year. April is the best time for performing this operation, after which they may receive an increase of water. They delight in a sandy soil not too rich. The bottom of every pot should be covered with an inch of broken pots or rough gravel for drainage.

CALADIUM ESCULENTUM (*Greenhouse Bulb, 35, 55, 85°*).

A beautiful, large decorative plant of most imposing appearance that will accommodate itself to various courses of treatment. As a pot plant, grown in the conservatory or window in winter, and removed to a place sheltered from winds in the summer, it grows to the height of four feet, and with its immense leaves lends a tropical appearance to collections, which is exceedingly effective. For garden culture the treatment suited to the Dahlia precisely meets the wants of this plant. It delights in a warm sandy soil, and may be left out until frosts cut down the foliage before taking up for the winter. As a single specimen pot plant it is without a superior, although somewhat subject to attacks of red spider. (See engraving, Fig. 36.)

Fig. 36. Caladium Esculentum.

CALANDRINIA (*Half-Hardy Annual*).

Free growing plants, producing heads of rosy, white and other colored flowers freely during the summer, that are desirable in the garden considering the slight expense and trouble necessary to rear them, although they cannot be classed among very fine flowers. They remain in flower until after frosts, and are frequently quite pretty thus late in the season. Sow in May where they are to flower, or earlier in heat or protected bed and transplant.

CALCEOLARIA—Carpet Bag or Moccasin Flower (*Greenhouse Perennials, 32, 45, 75°*).

Shrubby Calceolarias.—These are free blooming plants of good habits, which produce exceedingly novel and attractive flowers of irregular parts, the lower lip of each being a large inflated sac that presents an appearance which not inappropriately entitles it to the common name of Carpet Bag or Moccasin Flower. The plants are of erect shrubby habit, growing to a height of from one to two feet. They are valuable as pot plants in the window or conservatory, or for bedding out in positions that are shaded the hottest part of each day, as the intense heat of the sun in summer is not favorable to its growth and bloom. In the autumn they are the last to sustain injury from freezing, and can then be taken up and wintered in a well protected cold pit or cellar with ease. Also suitable for the conservatory or window in winter. Propagate from cuttings of the young growth. There are numerous varieties, but the following combine the greatest number of good points, all of which have pure, rich colors, and are of good form and size:

C. Aurea Floribunda, rich sulphur yellow. *C. Fulgens,* crimson maroon. *C. Golden Prince,* an excellent bright yellow. *C. Mrs. Woodruff,* deep crimson; large and brilliant; a tall grower. *C. Queen of Oude,* large crimson maroon, mottled in the most pleasing manner.

Herbaceous Calceolarias.—These belong to a distinct section of the family, being reared from seed sown in the greenhouse in the summer months, the plants flowering the following spring. Although the hybrid varieties are among the most showy plants in cultivation for decorating the conservatory, their culture would not be likely to result successfully in the window. The seeds are very fine and require careful treatment in sowing. As soon as the young seedlings can be handled they should be potted into small pots and given a place near the glass. Shift them into larger pots before the roots mat around the ball of earth, as their growth is liable to be checked if they become pot bound, and the green fly be invited. They require a rich sandy soil.

CALENDULA—Cape Marigold *(Hardy Annual).*

A desirable class of free growing annuals which flower almost continually throughout the summer and until after frosts, although some might consider them coarse, and with too few flowers.

C. La Prousti is a new double variety, of nankeen color, edged with brown. *C. Pluvialis,* single, white, of a remarkably pure color.

CALLA—Ethiopian Lily *(Greenhouse Perennial, 33, 45, 80°).*

Of all plants which are suitable for cultivating in pots in the window none are superior to the highly esteemed and easily managed Calla, while very few equal it. The same is true of its general value as a conservatory plant, excepting that it meets some rivals here which do not prove so formidable in the window garden, because few can be grown in the window to the magnificent perfection which this plant and its flowers reach. The flowers are large, pure white, and possess a delicate fragrance, which render them the very embodiment of purity and elegance. They are produced singly on long stems, and remain beautiful for several weeks. The plants bloom most freely in early spring, and are grown largely by florists for adorning churches at Easter, the flowers being exceedingly appropriate for this purpose. The best course of treatment for the Calla is, after they have flowered during fall, winter and spring, to give them a state of rest until August, by keeping the entire ball of soil next thing to dust-dry. At this time they should have the ball of earth thoroughly soaked, to facilitate washing the soil from the roots, which should be done, and small offsets be removed, after which the tuberous root should be potted in a rich soil, and given an abundance of water daily, until and all during their flowering season, up to their next annual rest. It is impossible to overdo the watering, to the injury of the plant, as its nature admits of its growing in water constantly, which renders it valuable for planting in aquariums. If the soil is of a clayey loam nature, all the better. The small offsets from the root may be potted for new stock. There are two varieties, the tall and the dwarf *(Calla Ethiopica Nana),* both of which have white flowers. The tall kind grows to the height of from two to three feet, and the dwarf from twelve to twenty inches, with a proportionate difference in the size of the flowers.

CALLIOPSIS, or COREOPSIS *(Hardy Annual).*

Annuals that produce an abundance of convenient long-stemmed flowers, throughout the season, of unusually rich bright colors, such as yellow and crimson, yellow and brown, velvety crimson, blood-red, yellow with crimson spots, etc. There are dwarf and tall varieties, the former growing from one to two feet, the latter, two feet and upwards. Of easy culture in any garden soil.

CAMELLIA *(Greenhouse Perennial, 32, 50, 75°).*

In the conservatory the Camellia is queen of winter flowers, and to the commercial florist during winter is valuable above all others for making bouquets, baskets of flowers, etc. It is well adapted to cultivation in the window, as regards the suitability of the situation, as the plant naturally grows in shady places in the woods, but to be successful in having it flower it requires strict attention to its peculiar wants in other respects. The plant produces its large flowers during the winter. They are from three to six inches in diameter, very pleasing and perfect in form, the petals being thick and of the most extraordinary satiny texture. The principal colors are pure (purest) white—the favorite color—bright rose, cherry color, scarlet rose, bright red variegated, salmon rose and others. After flowering, the Camellia makes its plant growth, preceding which time it should be re-potted, if at all. They require shifting but once every two years, except with very thrifty young plants, which may receive it each spring. Any soil is suited to its growth, provided it is well enriched with one-third part of leaf mould and thoroughly rotten manure. With its growth in spring, we meet with the distinct peculiarity of this plant, in forming its flower buds, *more than half a year previous to their opening* into flowers, and it is during the long time between which it forms its flower buds, and the season of their opening, that the treatment—either good or bad—which the plant receives, decides whether it will develop the buds, usually formed in abundance, into flowers, or whether they will drop from the plant some weeks before their time of opening, a condition of affairs, perhaps, most commonly met by inexperienced cultivators. Were the treatment it requires during this time difficult, there would be a good excuse for an unfortunate termination of the flower-buds, but this is by no means the case. The plant simply requires a light, shady place in summer, such as may be found in a shaded greenhouse that is well ventilated (see "Summer Management of the Amateur's Conservatory"), or in the shade of a building or verandah, and be given an abundance of water, also paying attention to cleanliness, of the thick leathery foliage. The plant will become dry enough to injure the flower-buds, without showing it, by the leaves drooping as in other plants. Its habit is deceitful in this respect, the leaves looking green and bright, although the soil is quite too dry for its general good, and especially for the flower-buds. The soil must, however, not be kept in a soaked condition, as this would prove as great an injury as the other. Water should be applied only when the surface becomes dry, and then a sufficient quantity should be poured on, to *entirely* soak the ball of earth, letting this suffice until the plant requires and is given another thorough watering, which may be the next day or later. During its flowering season water must not be spared, and in the dwelling the atmosphere should be kept as moist as practical. In the conservatory, that portion where the Camellias are kept, must have the glass shaded from the sun as soon in the spring as the plants start into growth, or else the leaves will become spotted. Keep a lookout for Red Spider on the leaves; these insects, although not particularly troublesome to this plant, sometimes makes inroads upon them before we are aware of their presence.

CAMPANULA *(Hardy Annuals and Perennials).*

The annual Campanulas are neat, free-flowering plants of small size; are useful for massing. The colors are not bright, and range from white to rosy purple and blue; should be sown where they are to bloom. The hardy section includes the well-known *Canterbury Bells* (Campanula Medium), which is readily grown from the seed, and other desirable sorts.

CANDYTUFT *(Hardy Annuals, Principally).*

The annual Candytuft is. one of the most useful plants that can be cultivated. It is grown from the seed with ease, and in a remarkably short time after sowing, the plant will start up and become completely covered with flowers, if the weather is warm. The same plants will not flower freely during the entire summer, and it is better to sow several times for succession, where an abundance of flowers are constantly desired. They will bloom until after frosts. The flowers are pure white, and several shades of crimson, and lilac, and are very suitable for bouquet-making. The seed may be sown very early in the spring. Thin out the plants to be four or six inches apart. The *Hardy Candytuft* (Iberis Sempervirens) is a hardy plant of spreading habit which produces an abundance of pure white flowers early in the spring. It does not die to the ground in winter, and should be somewhat protected to keep the foliage green; may be propagated by layers.

CANARY BIRD FLOWER. See Tropæolum.

CANNA *(Tender Bulbous Perennial).*

This is a genus of ornamental plants that are peculiarly adapted to the American climate. They thrive with the greatest vigor, either if grown in pots or bedded in the garden, and produce a stately tropical effect, with their broad massive foliage and beautiful flowers, under the most ordinary treatment and care. The Canna is freely propagated by division of the roots at planting time. During winter, the roots should be kept in sand in a dry cellar, or under the bench in the conservatory. Only the least showy sorts come well from seed, the really valuable varieties being shy seeders.

C. Bicolor, a beautiful free-growing variety, with a blending of various shades of green in the foliage. *C. Giganteus Aureantica*, foliage yellowish green, of fine appearance and free-growing habit. *C. Indica*, flowers scarlet, foliage green, free grower. *C. Tricolor*, is a variety of recent introduction, and is very desirable as a compact grower three feet high, with beautifully marked leaves. The stem, with the young terminal growth, and also leaf margins, are tinted with red, making an elegant contrast to the general effect of the foliage, which is densely streaked and mottled with creamy white. *C. Warzewiczi*, foliage striped with dark maroon-like crimson and green, the leaves growing eighteen inches long from the stalk, and eight or ten inches wide. I have measured clumps of this variety, grown from a single plant set out in spring, that were by September over four feet high, with leaves extending two feet from the center each way; a superior variety.

CARNATION—MONTHLY OR TREE *(Greenhouse Perennial, 27, 50, 85°).*

The Monthly Carnation I take pleasure in recommending to all cultivators of flowers, because but few plants possessing its hardiness and ease of culture have so many rare qualities. It is a rival of the Rose, the Japan Lily and other plants of equally high order. The flowers are deliciously fragrant, and possess, in the different varieties, colors unsurpassed in richness and beauty. The plants if set in spring bloom abundantly all summer in the flower garden, and plants properly prepared flower just as freely all during winter in the window or conservatory. For this latter named purpose they should be grown in the garden until the middle of September, removing all flower buds as they appear. (See Preparatory Treatment of Plants designed for Winter Flowering, page 14.) Some varieties are better adapted for winter flowering than others. . President Degrau, Edwardsii, La Purity, De Fontaine and Valliant generally are preferred for this purpose. In open ground plant not nearer than one foot apart; they may be propagated from layers of the branches or from cuttings.

Edwardsii, pure white, large. *De Fontaine*, yellow ground, edged with scarlet, white and crimson; extra. *Fortuneii*, crimson. *La Purity*, deep carmine, profuse and large flowering; very choice. *Louise Lenoir*, dark crimson. *Louis Zeller*, white. *President Degrau*, pure white; the best white for general purposes. *Solferino*, dark crimson scarlet. *Valliant*, small, bright scarlet, profuse bloomer. *Variegated La Purity*, carmine and white.

CARPET BAG OR MOCCASIN FLOWER. See Calceolaria.

CELOSIA—Cockscomb *(Half-Hardy Annual).*

A class of plants desirable in every collection on account of the singular and attractive

Fig. 37. Monthly Carnation Plant in Pot.   Fig. 38. Monthly Carnation Flower.

appearance and growth of the flowers.   They possess numerous good colors, scarlet or crimson being the most brilliant, and are exceedingly rich and showy.   The plants are grown from seed, which should be started in heat, and transplanted to the garden after frosts are over, as they are easily killed by freezing.   In the hot-bed or window give plenty of air to the young seedlings lest they dampen off or rot to the ground.   The plants, especially of the dwarf varieties, are admirably suited to pot culture in summer, thriving almost equal to those planted out, if the soil is rich and sandy.   Several new varieties of late years are attracting considerable attention.

CENTAUREA *(Greenhouse Perennial, 30, 45, 80°).*

An interesting and beautiful genus of white-foliaged ornamental plants that rank higher among the several distinct kinds possessing similar attractions than any other family; either when grown in pots, baskets or vases, or if bedded out, for which purpose they are not only generally valuable but exceedingly attractive, especially when used for planting at the edge of beds containing large growing Cannas, etc., or for contrasting with Coleus, Achryanthes, etc., in ribbon lines and masses.   They are easily grown, comparatively hardy, and few plants in our collections are more satisfactory to the cultivator.

C. Candida, a lovely plant of neat, compact, bushy growth, with exceedingly pretty silver-colored foliage.   *C. Gymnocarpa,* a variety with attractive cut foliage, of graceful semi-drooping habit.   It is one of the finest plants in cultivation for planting in the centre of hanging baskets, vases, etc., or for bedding out, being also more readily propagated then Candida.

CENTRADENIA *(Greenhouse Perennial, 35, 55, 95°).*

Beautiful, neat plants adapted only to window and conservatory culture in pots, or for planting in Ferneries, baskets, etc.   They delight in light soil, considerably enriched with leaf mould and manure.   Are propagated from cuttings.

C. Grandiflora, elegant narrow, green and crimson colored foliage, of changeable hue.   *C. Rosa,* small fine leaves, of pretty form and color.   The plant is profusely covered with small rose-colored flowers during a great portion of the year.

CENTURY PLANT.   See Agave.

CEREUS GRANDIFLORUS—NIGHT-BLOOMING CEREUS *(Greenhouse Perennial, 35, 50, 95°)*

The flowers of this celebrated kind of Cactus, which open only at *night time,* are very large, beautiful and sweet-scented.   They begin to open about sundown, and are fully expanded by eleven o'clock.   The petals are white; the coralla, or rather calyx, is from seven to ten inches in diameter, the outside of which is a brown and the inside a fine straw yellow color.   Its scent perfumes the air to considerable distance.   The plant is of thrifty habit, and is as easily grown to flower in the house or conservatory as any Cactus, requiring treatment similar to that described for this family.

CHOROZEMA ELEGANS *(Greenhouse Perennial, 32, 45, 80°).*

A small shrubby plant for pot culture, with dark green Holly-leaf shaped foliage, that will thrive and flower freely in any cool place in winter. The flowers are yellow and crimson, of pea shape, and attractive; one of the easiest plants to cultivate.

Fig. 39. Virgin Queen Chrysanthemum.

CHRYSANTHEMUM *(Hardy Perennial).*

The Chinese Chrysanthemums are exceedingly handsome late flowering plants, and although hardy in our latitude, the blossom buds are liable to be injured by hard fall frosts, unless protected somewhat. The best way to manage them is either to grow in pots during the summer, or take them up in September, and in either case remove to the house, where their many gorgeous flowers of various colors and tints will expand in succession for a long time. If grown in pots these should be plunged to the rim in the border; it is necessary to turn the pots occasionally to prevent the roots from striking through the bottom and growing in the garden soil. As they start into bud treat them to occasional waterings of liquid manure. After flowering the plants should be cut down and put in a cool part of the conservatory, in a cold-pit or in a light cellar, until spring. They may be increased in number either from cuttings of young shoots or by division of the roots in spring. The Chrysanthemums are especially recommendable to inexperienced cultivators, as no class of plants are easier to manage, and besides they produce their flowers late in autumn at a time when all kinds of flowers are scarce.

LARGE FLOWERING CHRYSANTHEMUMS.—*Aurora*, orange. *Cinderella*, pure white, fine. *Condrillion* various shades of orange and yellow. *Dr. Brooks*, rich golden yellow. *Empress of India*, clear white, large. *Fimbriata*, pure white, fimbriated, fine. *Gloric Mundi*, brilliant yellow. *Leonidas*, light crimson and orange. *Ne Plus Ultra*, rose; few flowers, but immense size. *Profusion*, deep blush. *Queen of Lilac*, light lilac. *Rosy Queen*, early, delicate rose, fine. *Virgin Queen*, snow white, very desirable (see Fig. 39). *Webb's Queen*, lilac. *White Trevenna*, pure white, medium size.

POMPONE, OR SMALL FLOWERING CHRYSANTHEMUMS.—*Alex. Peel*, cinnamon. *Apollo*, brilliant crimson. *Boule Blanche*, globe shape, white. *Bould de Neige*, white, yellow center. *Condrillion*, yellow, profuse. *Crouchon*, ruby red, excellent. *Fairy Nymph*, pure white. *Iona*, rosy lilac. *Jonas*, crimson and yellow. *La Brazier*, deep bronze. *Lilac Gem*, very dwarf, fine habit. *Mignonette*, rosy pink. *Prince Albert of Prussia*, white, fimbriated. *Roi des Lilliputs*, purple, white tipped. *Rosabelle*, deep rosy crimson.

JAPANESE CHRYSANTHEMUMS.—These are noted for their varied forms and markings, together with the enormous size which some of the varieties assume. *Grandiflora Japonica*, straw color, fringed. *Madam Chapon*, orange and yellow plated petals. *Richesse*, crimson.

CIGAR PLANT. See Cuphea Platycentra.

CINERARIA *(Greenhouse Perennial, 33, 45, 75°).*

In late winter and early spring, few plants in our conservatories present a more attractive appearance than do the Cinerarias when at their height of beauty, bearing an immense crop of bright, cheerful flowers, in clusters, boldly above the large, somewhat coarse looking, leaves. They are a capital class of plants for winter culture in a cool greenhouse, making a rapid growth; usually reared from seeds sown at any time from July to September. The culture suited to the Herbaceous Calceolarias (which see) will answer fully for the Cineraria, and any person may expect to be successful with their culture in the conservatory, also in the window, if a moist atmosphere can be sustained and they are kept near the light.

CISSUS DISCOLOR *(Greenhouse Perennial, 45, 65, 90°).*

A climber, with leaves beautifully shaded with dark green, purple and white, the upper surface of the leaf having a rich, velvet-like appearance. The plant requires a continual high temperature to develop the beautiful coloring of leaves, and there will be little use of attempting its culture unless this can be provided, and with this and other favorable conditions no plant in cultivation can exceed the rare beauty of its foliage.

CLARKIA *(Hardy Annual).*

Plants of considerable beauty for the garden that are easily reared from seed, which may be sown directly where they are to flower, either early in the spring or in August and September, by protecting the young seedlings, with a slight covering of straw or litter, which must be removed early the following spring. The flowers are attractive in form and color, with double and single varieties. They attain the greatest perfection in spring and autumn, as the hot sun of summer interferes somewhat with their development.

COBŒA SCANDENS *(Greenhouse Perennial, 35, 55, 85°).*

An excellent climbing plant, grown from seed or increased by layering, that is, perhaps, more generally useful than any other, being suitable for the conservatory, the window or the open air, but it requires careful management. The plants produce large, bell-shaped flowers freely in the open ground, but are rather shy in this respect when cultivated in pots, although their growth is satisfactory, and the foliage endures the confined heat of the dwelling admirably. When planted in a border, either in the conservatory or in a sheltered place out doors, the growth made by well established plants is enormous, having been known to reach a length of two hundred feet in one season. The seed require care in starting, which must be done in heat. Until the young plants appear, water very lightly—only enough to keep the soil from getting entirely dry. The Cobœa delights in a warm, sandy soil.

COCCOLOBA PLATYCLADA *(Greenhouse Perennial, 33, 50, 85°).*

A singular looking pot or bedding plant of fern-like, angular growth. It is readily grown, under most any circumstances, being also suitable for cultivating in ferneries, and is not out of place in a hanging basket. On account of its grotesque appearance, it will be admired where many flowering plants would scarcely attract attention. Propagates from cuttings.

COCKSCOMB. See Celosia.

COLEUS *(Greenhouse Perennial, 40, 60, 90°).*

This family possesses the most remarkable, varied and striking colors in their foliage of any plants in cultivation which are susceptible of being grown and propagated with equal ease. There is one condition, however, that is absolutely essential to its growth or even its existence, which is a high temperature, and where this is present, it will grow with the greatest freedom, either in the open air, the window or conservatory, and form strong plants of remarkable beauty in a very short space of time. The cultivator, meditating over a bed of beautiful Coleus in midsummer, each one of which has sprung up to form a large plant, from the small-sized one set out, perhaps, the first of June, can hardly realize that all this beauty is destined to fall under the first stroke of frost, be it ever so slight, to which it may be exposed later in the season. It is on account of this rapid growth, and withal their great beauty, that such vigorous varieties as Verschaffeltii, Setting Sun, Mutabilis and others, rank among the very best of plants for planting in masses or ribbon lines, even though tender they are. The majority of our dwellings that are heated by anthracite coal stoves or ranges, and in which fire heat is maintained day and night, will suit the Coleus if grown in pots or baskets and-placed in the light. A handsome size of plants may be reared for winter decoration by striking cuttings in July or August for the purpose. Plant them into light, rich soil and water moderately during winter, also pay attention to heading back strong growing shoots, to prevent a growth of "drawn" appearance.

C. Brunette, green leaves, spotted and blotched with various shades of maroon. *C. Canari*, a peculiar yellowish green variety, edged, and sometimes spotted, with maroon. *C. Chameleon*, a comparatively new and desirable variety, in which the colors of *pure rose*, green and purple are distinctly presented. *C. Edith*, rich dark red, edged with yellowish green. *C. Enchantress*, brilliant crimson and shades, edged with pale green. *C. Hamlet*, purplish maroon. *C. Hero*, chocolate maroon. *C. Mutabilis*, maroon and bronze, deeply edged with yellowish green. *C. Nonsuch*, light bronzy crimson, edged with green. *C. Princess of Prussia*, deep, velvety-crimson, the brightest variety in cultivation. *C. Princess of Wales*, purplish red, edged green. *C. Rainbow*, a blending of various colors, such as maroon, crimson, bronzy green, etc., in stripes and blotches. *C. Refulgent*, dark maroon; a strong grower. *C. Rival*, dark claret crimson, light green edge. *C. Setting Sun*, bronze crimson center, bright golden margin. *C. Shah*, recently introduced, the leaves, which are rich cinnamon, are marked the entire width and one-third or one-half their depth with golden yellow, although it is inclined to vary occasionally from this rule. *C. Verschaffeltii*, rich velvety crimson, of superior quality, either for bedding or pot culture.

COLUMBINE. See Aquilegia.

CONVOLVULUS (*Half-Hardy Annual*).

CONVOLVULUS MAJOR (Morning Glory).—A climbing plant that is perhaps as well known as any plant in cultivation, being excellent for covering trellises, rustic work, cords for shading the veranda, etc. There are many varieties of different colors, all of which are more or less attractive. The seed may be sown in the open ground quite early in the spring. As soon as the young plants stretch forth for support on which to spin, it should be provided, as they do not hold on so readily after being older, besides they become entangled with each other.

CONVOLVULUS MINOR (Dwarf Convolvulus). —Free flowering annuals of distinct and rich colors, that are desirable for massing or for individual effect. The seeds germinate readily, and may be sown where they are to flower. Thin out the plants to stand not nearer than fifteen inches apart in rich soil.

CROWN IMPERIAL (*Hardy Bulb*).

An old fashioned, early spring flowering bulb, bearing on a stem several feet high, drooping bell-shaped flowers, which in their arrangement around the stalk may be fancied to resemble a crown. There are both double and single varieties, the colors of which are principally yellow and red. They delight in a deep rich bed, and should not have their bulbs lifted for resetting oftener than every third year.

Fig. 40.   Cuphea Platycentra—Cigar Plant.

CUPHEA PLATYCENTRA—CIGAR PLANT (*Greenhouse Perennial, 32, 45, 80°*).

This is a pretty, shrub-like plant adapted to a variety of purposes. The flowers, which are tubular in form (see Fig. 40), are uniformly of a *bright* scarlet color, tipped at their opening with pure white and jet black edges. It is almost constantly in bloom under any fair circumstances, and will thrive beautifully as a hanging basket or vase plant, or if planted out in the border and beds, where it will during the season assume a dense globular form, and constantly produce hundreds of flowers. It is also valuable as a pot plant for the window, where its constantly appearing flowers of pleasing appearance will be certain to make it a favorite. The Cuphea is readily propagated from cuttings of the young growth.

CRASSULA COCCINEA (*Greenhouse Perennial, 34, 45, 85°*).

A plant suitable for the window or conservatory, which produces scarlet wax-like flowers of considerable beauty for a long time; should be kept rather dry during winter.

CROCUS *(Hardy Bulb).*

The Crocuses are an interesting class of bulbous plants, that produce their flowers in the open air through the month of April and up to the flowering of Hyacinths. Being very early, they are entitled to a place in every garden. The flowers are principally white, blue, yellow and striped, and present an exceedingly gay appearance, as they appear without a companion scarcely at their early season of flowering. The bulbs require to be planted in the fall, and should be set about three inches apart and not more than two inches deep. Their culture, in common with other hardy bulbs, is generally treated on on page 14. The Crocus will also flower well in the house. Directions for cultivation in glasses, pots, etc., is given on page 21.

CYCLAMEN PERSICUM *(Greenhouse Bulb, 35, 55, 75°).*

Beautiful plants for the conservatory, with delicately marked foliage, which produce from autumn until spring a profusion of small bell-shaped flowers of the most pleasing appearance, on long stems. The soil in which they are potted should be very rich. After they have done flowering, they may be kept plunged in the open ground during summer and receive a shift into larger pots for flowering, in August or September. The plants are reared from seed, which may be sown at any time from early spring until mid-summer, for flowering the next year.

CYPRESS VINE. See Ipomœa.

CYTISUS RACEMOSUS *(Greenhouse Perennial, 35, 50, 80°).*

Cytisus Racemosus is a winter flowering pot plant, suitable for the window or conservatory, assuming an irregular bushy form, which is very attractive. The flowers are small, very sweet, and of a pleasing, deep golden yellow color, borne on racemes that, for a long time, give the plant a beautiful appearance. It is difficult to propagate.

DAFFODIL. See Narcissus.

DAHLIA *(Tender Tuber).*

Well known tuberous plants, only suitable for open-air culture, which produce flowers of the most perfect and beautiful form, and of unexceptionally brilliant and good colors, during the summer and autumn months. Luxuriate in a moist soil. In dry weather the flowers will be finer, and the plants do better, by receiving a thorough watering occasionally of an evening. Nothing gives Dahlias a better appearance than to keep them neatly tied to strong stakes about four feet long, one driven in the ground by each plant. All flowers should be removed as soon as they begin to decay, and imperfect buds be cut off. The tubers are to be lifted after frosts have killed the stalk, usually the forepart of October in our latitude. They should then be labeled, and after having been allowed to dry, either in the sun or in an open shed, packed in sand and kept in a dry, warm cellar during winter or under the benches in the conservatory; after the middle of May they may be divided in pieces, each with a crown, and planted in the flower beds again. Their flowering season is considerably advanced by starting and keeping them growing in the hot-bed, up to near the first of June; for this purpose start in April.

Amazement, dark crimson.
Belle de Baum, deep pink.
Bob Ridley, dark scarlet.
Black Dwarf, dark maroon.
Col. Sherman, light scarlet.
Criterion, delicate rose color.
Celestial, bluish lilac.
Dr. Stein, dark maroon with light blotches.
Deutschland's Ehre, red, tipped with pale rose.
Eugenie, white, tipped with scarlet.
Fulgens Picta, scarlet, tipped white.
Glory of Summer, rich glowing salmon.
Golden Fleece, yellow, tipped pink.
Goldfinder, golden yellow.
Grand Duke, large lilac.
Grimaldi, large and attractive.
Guiding Star, pure white, fimbriated.
Little Kate, small maroon.
Little Model, rosy crimson, light center.
Little Virginie, bright rosy purple.

Mandarin, clear yellow, pale rose stripe.
Magician, crimson and white.
Main Strefling, salmon, striped crimson.
Miss Amarang, dwarf crimson.
Mrs. Seacole, an excellent variety.
Norah Crinea, orange, tipped white.
Paradise Williams, clear claret.
Pearl, pure white.
Penelope, blush, purple tint.
Princess Calibri, deep scarlet.
Princess Alice, pale rose, with light center.
Princess of Prussia, blush and purple.
Queen of Sports, blush, spotted and streaked with purple.
Salvator Rosa, clear pink, fine form.
Selmer, yellow, purple tip.
Silver Fish.
Tom Green, maroon, tipped white.
Vedette, soft purple.
Venus, blush white.

DAISY—BELLIS PERENNIS *(Hardy Herbaceous Perennial).*

A pretty little plant for the garden, which bears a profusion of perfectly double flowers, of red, white, and red and white variegated colors, throughout all but the hottest portion of the season. They propagate by division and also from the seed, but are not very satisfactory if thus reared, as a large proportion always will come single or only semi-double from the best of seed. Set the plants about six inches apart, and protect slightly in winter. A few may be potted in the fall to flower in a cool place in the window or conservatory during winter.

4

DELPHINIUM—LARKSPUR *(Hardy Annuals and Perennials).*

ANNUAL DELPHINIUMS.—A class of annuals possessing bright colors and free flowering qualities that are worthy of culture in every considerable garden collection. The dwarf varieties are regarded as the most beautiful. They attain a height of one foot, throwing up a flower shoot that somewhat resembles a Hyacinth. These should stand at a distance of six inches from each other, and the tall varieties a foot and a half apart. Sow where they are to bloom.

DELPHINIUM FORMOSUM is one of the most desirable hardy perennial plants in cultivation. It blooms more or less freely from July until November, giving a supply of exceedingly attractive flowers. The flowers are large, lively blue, with the center white, shaded with reddish purple. When the plants become large they should be divided and reset; they can also be grown true from seed, which should be sown in spring, and will flower the next summer.

Fig. 41. Diadem Pink (Dianthus Heddewigii Diadematus fl. pl.).

DEUTZIA *(Hardy Shrub).*

Although a family of hardy shrubs, and one of the best for permanent planting, the varieties *Deutzia Gracilis,* pure white, and *Deutzia Gracilis fl. pl.,* double, pure white, serve admirably for pot culture and forcing into flower in the window or conservatory. The plants should be grown in the open ground, and after the leaves have fallen in autumn, be brought into the cold-pit or cellar, until New Year's, after which time they may be taken to the window or conservatory for flowering. With bearing a profusion of pretty flowers in due time, nothing can be handsomer.

DIANTHUS *(Hardy Perennial).*

This is an extensive genus of desirable flowering plants, which embrace numerous important kinds, the Carnation, Garden Pink, Sweet William, etc., being of the number. I shall here treat of those that are generally reared from seed, the others will be found under their respective heads. The species known as *D. Chinensis,* embracing the old Chinese Pink, very much improved of late years, and the new and superb varieties from Japan, known as *D. Heddewigii* and *lacinatus,* with the new varieties springing from them through the means of hybridization (see illustration of Diadem Pink, Fig. 41), are among the most brilliant and useful of garden flowers. They are easily reared from seed in any good soil, and flower freely during the season, even up to winter, and for several years, provided they are in suitable condition for surviving the winter. It is better to secure strong, stocky plants by pruning, even at the expense of some bloom, by fall, as they will not only winter better but will produce larger and finer flowers the second season. The seed may be sown in heat and the young plants transplanted, if large plants are desired the first year, or by sowing in the garden at any time from late spring until September, excellent plants may be had for flowering the following year. The plants should be set at a distance of from six to twelve inches apart.

Fig. 42. Tricolor Geranium, Mrs. Pollock. See page 57.

DIANTHUS BARBATUS *(Sweet William)*, useful garden perennials, with double and single varieties of various colors. They have long been in cultivation, but great improvements have been made in the quality of the flowers, as well as in the increase of desirable varieties. Easily raised from seeds, or fine varieties may be perpetuated by dividing the roots after they have flowered.

DICENTRA SPECTABILIS—LOVE LIES BLEEDING *(Hardy Herbaceous Perennial).*

One of our most ornamental, spring-flowering hardy herbaceous plants, and also excellent for forcing in the window or conservatory. The flowers appear in racemes, on long drooping stems, are of a bright róse pink, with pearly white corolla, and as they are produced by hundreds on large plants in the open air, rendering the plant for the time one of the most attractive objects the garden will contain during the season. For winter flowering they should be taken up in October, potted, and placed in a cold-pit or some place where they may be got at in winter. Any time after cold weather sets in (they should have a freeze) they may be brought indoors and will flower in about two months.

DIGITALIS—Fox Glove *(Hardy Biennial).*

A well known hardy border plant, flowering in June and July, possessing considerable beauty. The flowers in the different varieties are purple, white and spotted; have a thimble-like shape, and are produced in dense spikes. Are propagated by sowing the seed in the spring or up to the middle of August, and flower the second year.

DRACENA *(Greenhouse Perennial, 35, 60, 95°).*

Tropical plants of rare beauty, only suited to pot or Fernery culture in the window or conservatory, but may be introduced in summer decoration, in pots, vases and hanging baskets with grand effect. The beauty of the plant consists in the leaves, which range in color from various shades of green to bright crimson and pink, striped with dark green in the different varieties, and are long, narrow and straight, somewhat resembling those of the Indian Corn plant, except that they are shorter. Do best in soil consisting of one-third part leaf mould, also containing some sand, and kept pretty moist.

ECHEVERIA *(Greenhouse Perennial, 35, 50, 90°).*

A remarkable class of plants, with thick succulent leaves of grotesque appearance, suitable for pot culture in the window or conservatory, and also for bedding. They are prized chiefly for their odd, yet, in some varieties, delicate appearance, as few would consider them possessed of any greater beauty than that found in plants of the Cactus family. They are of the easiest culture, and while delighting in moisture generally, should be kept quite dry during winter.

ERYSIMUM PEROFFSKIANUM *(Hardy Annual).*

A free flowering little annual producing flowers of beautiful orange shade, which are esteemed for their sweetness and suitability for cutting. Sow the seed where it is to flower.

ESCHOLTZIA CALIFORNICA—California Poppy *(Hardy Annual).*

The Escholtzia is a desirable garden annual easily grown from seed, and flowers almost continually from June until cold weather. The flowers are of a splendid rich, deep yellow color in *E. Californica*, which cultivators generally consider the best, and possess a dazzling brilliancy in the sunshine. Their dense growth should be supported by sticks, else a portion of the plant will lie close to the ground, detrimental to their perfect flowering. Sow where they are to flower and thin out to one foot.

EUONYMUS *(Greenhouse Perennial, 30, 45, 90°).*

Very beautiful plants of shrubby nature, valuable for pot culture, Ferneries, winter hanging baskets, and in fact for any in-door purpose, as they are of neat, vigorous habit, with lovely variegated leaves of glossy Ivy-like texture, and are scarcely equaled for growing in the shade.

The varieties are *Aurea variegata* and *Radicans variegata*, which are nearly alike, except in their colors. The leaves of the former are a rich golden yellow color on green; and in *Radicans variegata*, a bright pea green, deeply margined with creamy white, both having a striking and pretty appearance, not found in any similar plant.

EUPATORIUM *(Greenhouse Perennial, 33, 45, 75°).*

This is a family of plants extensively grown by florists for the abundant crop of pure white flowers they produce only in winter. The flowers are borne in dense clusters on good stems. The plant is vigorous, of upright habit, and requires considerable pot room; of the easiest culture under any circumstances. As it propagates readily, it is best to start young plants early each spring for flowers the following winter; they should be grown in pots out of doors in a place protected from wind, during summer. Cut down the plants after flowering, which will induce a new growth to propagate from.

There are three varieties generally cultivated, the flowers of which are white and nearly alike in appearance. *E. Arboreum* is the earliest to flower, *E. Salicifolius* (very pure white) next, and *E. Elegans* latest, the three varieties affording a succession of bloom during the winter.

EVERLASTING FLOWERS. See Acroclinium, Amobium Helichrysum, Helipterum, Gomphrena, Rhodanthe, and Xeranthemum.

FABIANA IMBRICATA *(Greenhouse Perennial, 34, 50, 90°).*

One of the prettiest little shrub-like pot plants that can be cultivated, being of dense pyramidal habit, fine foliage and profusely covered with white flowers in spring; excellent for baskets in summer or winter. Any ordinary treatment and good soil will suit this plant.

FARFUGIUM GRANDE *(Greenhouse Perennial, 35, 50, 90°).*

A singular looking plant of easy culture in the window or conservatory, the leaves of which are its attractive feature. These are large, round, borne on long stems, are smooth, of a deep green color, and blotched with distinct golden yellow spots, ranging from the size of a pin's head to nearly an inch across and distributed with a striking irregularity over the surface. They are increased by new shoots starting from the root, which should be potted. Suitable for planting in baskets, vases, etc.

FERN *(Greenhouse Perennial, 35, 45 or 50, 80°).*

There are many varieties of Ferns or Brakes found growing in wood and swamp lands, in all parts of our country. These are principally of kinds whose roots continue to live from year to year—the tops dying annually. There are numerous varieties grown in greenhouses, differing from these inasmuch as the foliage is perennial or evergreen, thus being continually attractive, summer and winter. This class are among the most attractive plants which can be grown under glass or in the window, and especially in the latter, with the use of a Fernery or plant case. On page 19 this means of growing plants is treated upon, and I will repeat that it exactly suits the wants of Ferns and many other plants of similar requirements. Ferns are propagated from the spores which form on the leaves, these being sown in earth similar to seeds of seed bearing plants, a somewhat difficult and uncertain means of propagation, with which few amateurs would be successful, for want of suitable appliances. The plants should be grown in soil largely composed of leaf mould from the woods.

FEVERFEW—PYRETHRUM *(Greenhouse Perennial, 33, 45, 85°).*

Very useful bedding plants in several varieties, all of which are nearly hardy, of the easiest possible culture and readily propagated from cuttings. The double white Feverfew (Pyrethrum Parthenum) produces an immense crop of perfectly double, pure white, daisy-like flowers, an inch and upwards in size, in clusters, on stems eighteen inches high, the fore part of summer, and then less freely at intervals, until late in the season, on which account it has become an important plant in every florist's greenhouse, and is deserving of general cultivation at the hands of amateurs, especially as there need be no failure with managing it to produce an abundance of bloom.

Prince Alfred is a variety similar to the preceding but of dwarfer habit. *Golden Feather Feverfew* possesses no merit as a flowering plant, but is highly esteemed for its attractive, delicate cut foliage of greenish golden color, and the dense symmetrical growth it assumes. It is a beautiful plant for massing or planting in ribbon lines and, like the two varieties described above, is very suitable as a pot plant or for planting in vases and large hanging baskets. The flower shoots should be pinched back as they appear. All the Feverfews may be taken from the ground in fall and wintered in a cold-pit. To rear an abundance of stock for bedding, take plants thus secured, into heat in February and then make cuttings of the young shoots.

FORGET-ME-NOT. See Myosotis.

FOUR O'CLOCK. See Mirabilis Jalapa.

FOX GLOVE. See Digitalis.

FUCHSIA—LADY'S EAR DROP *(Greenhouse Perennial, 35, 50, 85°).* See Fig. 43.

The Fuchsia is another of those superb families of plants, the varieties of which, to an extent, are indispensable in every collection of choice plants. It is a well known genus, and has for years attracted the attention of cultivators by its elegant appearance and lovely flowers. The Lady's Ear Drop, as it is commonly called, is associated with our earliest recollection of window plants, cultivated many years ago, but since that time, like with many other things, the florist's art of hybridizing has caused wonderful changes and improvements in the flowers, and has rendered the varieties of to-day immensely superior to those known a score of years ago. The Fuchsia is admirably adapted for pot culture on the window-shelf or in the conservatory— some varieties flowering beautifully in the winter. They delight not so much in a high temperature as in a light place in which they can frequently be treated to fresh air. Their nature requires a season of rest annually, which should be given the ordinary varieties from the latter part of summer until January, and the winter blooming kinds for several months in summer. During this time water should be withheld from the plants to an extent that will cause the leaves to drop, a little being applied occasionally to prevent the soil from becoming entirely dry. They may be placed in any dry, airy place, but in the winter not where it freezes. After they have rested sufficiently, they should be cut back to a degree that will encourage the formation of a well formed plant from the new growth, and should be well supplied with water. As the flower buds appear, plants may receive an occasional watering with liquid manure. Frequently repotting the plants as they require it into larger sized pots, and in a soil of the most fertile nature—it may be one-half well rotted manure—are important in growing the plant to perfection. By paying attention to this, and supplying sufficient water, a growth of an astonishing magnitude and appearance may be had in the time of a few months, by starting with a good healthy young plant. Excellent as a flowering plant in the center of hanging baskets and vases, and the double varieties are quite suitable for bedding in a partially shaded place protected from sweeping winds.

Alba coccinea, sepals white; corolla violet, mottled with rose ; tube streaked with dark pink. *Arabella,* white tube and sepals ; corolla rich rose. *Aurora Superba,* rich, waxy pink ; splendid habit. *Avalanche* (Smith's), tube and sepals carmine ; corolla deep violet, and exceedingly large and double ; a free grower and profuse bloomer ; regarded as one of the finest double varieties. *Bianca,* white sepals ; deep pink corolla. *Bianca marginata,* early, free flowering ; the sepals are white and finely reflexed ; corolla delicate pink ; a handsome branching, erect grower. *Bridesmaid,* sepals white ; dark pink corolla. *Brilliant,* corolla bright scarlet ; sepals

Fig. 43. Double Fuchsias—Avalanch and Princess of Wales.

white. *Charming*, violet corolla; crimson sepals, immense clusters. *Criterion*, coral-red tube and sepals; blue corolla. *Dagmar*, a fine and distinct variety; the tubes and sepals are crimson; corolla rosy violet, laying open in peculiar salver-shaped form. *Elm City*, tube and sepals crimson scarlet; corolla dark purple, double; an early flowering and desirable variety. *Evening Star*, sepals blush; corolla crimson scarlet. *Fulgens*, a variety of peculiar form, having a small bright scarlet tube, enlarging to a pencil-like diameter at about three inches from its stem, where it divides into four white-pointed sepals; the corolla is also scarlet; novel and beautiful. *Geo. Felton*, crimson scarlet sepals and tube; dark purple corolla; very double. *Grandiflora Gem*, a very desirable variety; the tube and sepals are light crimson; corolla dark crimson; fine form and large size. *Heather Bell*, tube and sepals white; corolla dark crimson; quite distinct. *Little Dorrit*, a variety of miniature size; tube and general form about one-fourth the ordinary size; very free flowering. *Puritani*, white corolla; scarlet sepals. *Prince Imperial*, sepals fine scarlet; corolla violet; the earliest dark variety. *Princess of Wales*, a crimson scarlet variety of glossy texture, with white corolla; very double and large. *Rose of Castile*, sepals white; corolla violet rose; a somewhat dwarf, but early and profuse bloomer; one of the best. *Sally Mead*, tube and sepals scarlet; corolla crimson; very double and of irregular length, laying open like a rose. *Sir Colin Campbell*, an old favorite; double; tube and sepals scarlet; corolla dark purple. *Schiller*, sepals white; corolla a light violet, changeable to rose; a profuse and early bloomer. *Victor Emanuel*, tube and sepals coral red; corolla fine double white, tinted with scarlet stripes; beautiful. *Wave of Life*, golden foliage; sepals scarlet; corolla dark purple. *White Eagle*, corolla white; sepals carmine.

WINTER FLOWERING FUCHSIAS.—The following two varieties are the best for winter flowering, while Bianca Marginata is also useful for this purpose. *Carl Halt*, a new and distinct variety, and very valuable for winter flowering. The flower is striped in clear colors of white and red, in a novel and beautiful form; very productive. *Speciosa*, a well known variety, producing large flowers two inches in length, tubes and sepals of which are blush, the corolla crimson. The single plants of this variety, grown in eight or nine inch pots, will produce from three hundred to five hundred flowers from December to May.

FUNKIA—THE DAY LILY *(Hardy Herbaceous Perennial).*

The White Day Lily *(F. Alba Odora)* is an attractive, bulbous garden plant, with luxuriant, broad, ovate, veined foliage of rich yellowish green color, that grows in an elegant clump or mass one foot high. The flowers are pure white and fragrant, of an exceedingly pleasing appearance, and are borne on stems twenty inches high, before midsummer, opening only in the day. A mass of this beautiful plant growing on the lawn is very handsome. *F. Cærulea*, quite similar to the above, excepting that the flowers are light blue, and the foliage of a deep green. *F. Marginata*, with elegant variegated leaves, distinctly edged and striped with sulphur yellow.

GALANTHUS—SNOWDROP *(Hardy Bulbous Perennial).*

Most delightful little flowers, blooming in the open air the very earliest of all flowers, generally in warm, sunny exposures long before the snow has all disappeared. There are double and single varieties, pure white. No garden can be considered fairly stocked, without at least a few clumps of these earliest of early flowers. The bulbs should be planted in the fall months with Hyacinths, Tulips, etc., about two or three inches deep, and if set three inches apart in clumps a foot or two across, the effect will be the finest. Reset them once in three years. The Galanthus are also useful for forcing into bloom in winter. (See page 21).

GAZANIA *(Greenhouse Perennial, 32, 45, 85°).*

Summer and autumn flowering bedding plants of low prostrate habit; the prevailing colors are orange and yellow, with a broad, intensely black velvety ring passing around the center. Excellent for planting in hanging baskets and vases. Propagate from cuttings and layers.

GERANIUM—PELARGONIUM *(Greenhouse Perennials, 33, 45, 85°, except where noted).*

An extensive, varied and interesting family of plants of great value for pot culture and bedding; indeed, in such a degree, that a nice flower and window garden might be sustained by employing no other plants than those included in the genus. Their requirements throughout are of the most simple kind, and there is scarcely such thing as failure in realizing satisfaction from cultivating them, even by inexperienced amateurs. All the varieties of the several sections strike root readily from cuttings. August and September are suitable months for propagating, as an abundance of growth is then available, and cuttings struck at this season will make strong plants for next year's use. They will also, each, afford several young cuttings during the winter for propagation. Young plants make such rapid growth that it is better to provide plenty of new stock each fall and winter for bedding in the spring, and also for pot culture, to the exclusion of old plants. A light place, where air can be introduced to them, is most suitable for their winter quarters. Old plants can easily be kept over in a warm cold-pit or light cellar which is not too damp. (See Pelargonium.)

ZONALE, SCARLET, OR HORSESHOE GERANIUMS.—This is perhaps the best known class in cultivation, being easily grown, afford a large variety of colors, and different habits. As bedding plants they are unequaled, being rapid growers and are remarkably free-flowering. Scarcely a more pleasing or yet more simple disposal of plants can be effected than to mass the scarlet varieties a foot or eighteen inches apart, according to size, in a bed upon the lawn, to be viewed from a distance, as from a walk, or a favorite window in the living room. For brilliancy the varieties Gen. Grant and Queen of the West are the best, being strong growers and immense bloomers. All during the season many large dazzling heads of bloom will be conspicuous over the green, compact mass of leaves, affording a continual, never-tiring view for months, which, for attractiveness, cannot be fully approached by any other plants in cultivation, similarly arranged. The number of plants employed, or the size of the bed, has less to do with its general effectiveness, than, that only one variety be planted, and that of plants nearly uniform in size (see "Planting in Masses of Color," page 10). Varieties of other colors are quite as suitable for bedding in masses; my advice to amateurs, however, is, to make their first choice of the above-named varieties for this purpose, leaving other colors for subsequent plantings, unless it is desired to plant a compound bed with Geraniums, each part with a distinctly colored variety. The following varieties are best of this section for massing:

Gen. Grant, scarlet.   *Mons. Barre,* salmon rose.   *Pearl,* white.
Glorie de Carbonay, salmon pink.   *Mrs. Whitty,* deep pink.   *Queen of the West,* orange scarlet.

In massing Geraniums, the beds may or may not be edged with plants of showy foliage, as best suits the planter. The ground should always be slightly raised in the center and finished to a mound-like form. This class of Geraniums are much used as pot plants and for planting in the center of hanging baskets, urns and vases. For flowering in winter they should be pinched back occasionally during the previous summer, and not allowed to flower much.

Andrew Henderson, salmon, with scarlet tinted center; a beautiful variety.

Bicolor, flowers nearly pure white, with center markings of a rich, deep shade of rose.

Bridesmaid, salmon rose.

Blue Bells, color not a blue, but is a rich shade of majenta pink; forms an immense truss.

Col. Holden, attractive, deep rosy crimson.

Excellent, orange scarlet; a superior variety for pot or basket culture.

Francis Dubois, white, salmon center; extra.

Father Ignatius, extra large scarlet, of astonishing size and perfection.

General Grant, dazzling scarlet, immense truss, and very free-flowering.

General Ulot, large scarlet; very desirable.

Glorie de Carbonay, rich salmon pink; compact.

Glorious, brilliant scarlet.

Harlequin, a distinctly striped variety, ground color salmon pink, mottled and striped white.

Harold, brilliant scarlet, a free bloomer and compact grower.

Jean Sisley, a very desirable variety, of dwarf habit, flowers brilliant scarlet, with a distinct white eye.

Jennie, rosy pink; dwarf.

King of Pinks, neat, compact habit, with a dark, almost black-brown zone.

Laviata, very scarlet; a superb variety.

Little Gem, deep, clear scarlet, distinct white eye; novel and beautiful.

L'Incomparable, ground a clear salmon color, streaked with white; neat habit.

Louis Veronillot, deep crimson scarlet, fine form; very distinct and attractive.

Mad. Vaucher, pure white, compact grower.

Mad. Rendatler, pink; profuse.

Maid of Kent, color majenta, or lake rose.

Marginata, white; petals edged with pink.

Master Christine, very profuse dwarf; flowers deep rose, with white eye.

Mons. Barre, salmon rose, deep zone.

Mrs. Whitty, deep pink nosegay, a beautiful and desirable color; excellent.

Prince of Wales, salmon, light edge.

Pearl, pure white; excellent habit.

Queen of the West, bright orange; extra fine.

Rival, rich scarlet; a superior variety.

Sheen Rival, scarlet, tri-color-like foliage.

Snowball, pure white

Sparkler, crimson; immense truss, containing one hundred and upwards of flowers.

Troubadour, crimson scarlet; fine.

Warrior, large, bright scarlet; fine flower, and a good, well-shaped grower; finely zoned.

Wonder, carmine crimson, ornamental foliage.

DOUBLE GERANIUMS (see Figs. 44 and 45).—The Double Geraniums have been in cultivation for only a few years comparatively, but at the present time they include numerous desirable colors, even to pure white, with the introduction of Aline Sisley. Their general growing habit and appearance is similar to the common Zonale or Scarlet Geraniums, except that they have larger leaves on an average, and are something stronger in their growth, while the plants are equally valuable, whether employed for bedding or for growing in pots, but of course they are finer and more desirable for the latter purpose than the single kinds, because the flowers embrace the same distinct colors, are of fine texture, *as perfectly double as a Rose,* and are produced in the greatest profusion under ordinary treatment. The soil for them should not be as rich as for single Geraniums, as their growth, which is always inclined to be free, would become too rank, and less flowers would be the result.

Aline Sisley, this is a long desired acquisition, being a pure white, double Geranium of good, healthy and free-flowering habit. Still we must enjoy the florets while they are young, because, although perfectly white, they do not remain so for more than a few days, after which they assume a pinkish tint. I trust this variety is the forerunner of others, whose color will continue white, like the single varieties. *Ascendency,* light rose; vigorous. *Double Andrew Henderson,* dark scarlet, large truss, fine flower and good grower. *Duc de Suez,* very double scarlet crimson, the largest of all double varieties yet introduced; flowers of excellent shape, imbricated and of immense size; habit of the plant compact and neat; free-flowering, beautiful and distinct. *Emile Lemoine,* fine truss and pips; color light orange scarlet, very attractive. *Jeanne de St. Maur,* bright vermillion. *Madame Lemoine,* the color of this variety is a beautiful rose of the most pleasing shade and is admired by every one; a free bloomer, fine truss and form; good healthy grower, and in every way a first-class plant. *Princess Teck,* a variety producing very large, bright scarlet flowers; perfectly double and beautiful; very excellent and desirable in every collection. *Triumph,* rich shade of scarlet. *Triumph de Lorraine,* bright cherry carmine. *Wm. Pfitzer,* a scarlet flowering, dwarf variety.

Fig. 44. Double Geranium Plant.   *Fig. 45. Double Geranium Flower.*

IVY-LEAVED GERANIUMS (Peltatum).—In this beautiful division we are given habits of drooping and climbing character, adapting them admirably for planting at the edges of vases and
baskets for drooping over or for training to trellises in pot culture. The foliage in nearly all the
varieties is variegated, and of peculiar waxy texture, possessing mostly the Ivy-leaf shape. The
flowers are produced in abundance and show to delightful advantage, owing to the habit of the
plant. An interesting plant for bedding, as they grow freely and creep beautifully if not
supported.

Bridal Wreath, fine, large trusses of pure white flowers; very distinct. *Duke of Edinburgh,*
a new, large leaved variety. *Floribunda,* bright, glossy green, narrow zone, clearly variegated in
creamy white and green; pink flowers. *Holly Wreath,* deep and ragged golden white margin.
light green center. *L'Elegante,* deep pea green, with margin of white; very beautiful; this
excellent variety should be in every collection; will be certain to please. *Princess Alexandria,*
beautiful pure white flowers. *Remarkable,* a remarkably distinct variety of a more *decidedly
climbing habit* than any of the preceding varieties; leaves marked with a dark Vandyke ivy-
shaped zone, and flower truss is of a rich warm rose-colored bloom; well adapted for pot culture
and training to a trellis or conservatory pillar and for summer decoration in balconies.

TRICOLOR, GOLD AND SILVER-EDGED GERANIUMS *(35, 50, 85°),* see Fig. 46.—As their
names imply, the chief merit of this section consists in the distinctly edged and variegated foliage, although, without an exception, they produce fine flowers. Well grown specimens as
pot plants are exceedingly unique for decorating the parlor or conservatory, but they should
have a position as near the glass as possible, as the colors will be more clearly defined for being
thus treated. The different varieties are useful for planting on ribbon beds to contrast with
Coleus, Achryanthes, etc., or for edging to beds of Scarlet Geraniums; are also valuable for
planting in baskets and vases.

Attraction, leaves striped and edged with silver, bronze zone; flowers scarlet. *Avalanch,*
the new silver-edged Geranium, quite similar to Mount of Snow, except that the flowers are pure
white. *Beauty of Caulderdale,* yellowish green ground, fine dark zone; flowers scarlet. *Black
Hawk,* immense bronze band on light green; scarlet. *Crystal Palace Gem,* golden foliage, with
green diverging in marks from the center. *Cloth of Gold,* foliage golden yellow, with dark green
markings; scarlet flowers. *Flower of Spring,* a beautiful plant; leaves edged with straw-tinted
white; a free-growing variety; excellent either for pot or basket culture, or for bedding. *Golden
Fleece,* clear yellow leaves, tinted green. *Golden Pheasant,* margin golden yellow, fine zone;
scarlet. *Italia Unita,* sulphur white zone on the notched-like intersections
of green and white, being on the green a dark maroon color, on the white a rose and delicate
pink; scarlet flowers. *Lady Cullum,* finely-marked foliage, much like Mrs. Pollock. *Mount
of Snow,* pure white-margined foliage; scarlet flowers; strong grower; this is one of the best
and most desirable varieties of the class (see Fig. 46). *Mrs. Pollock,* one of the most beautiful

Fig. 46.—*Silver-edged Geranium.* (See Flower of Spring, Mount of Snow, etc., varieties.)

of the tri-colors; leaves colored with deep green, light green, crimson bronze and clear yellow; flowers deep scarlet (see Fig. 42). *Neatness*, greenish yellow, with broad chocolate band; cherry pink. *Rose Queen*, margined white, distinct zone on green disc. *Silver Pheasant*, leaves margined with tinted white; compact grower.

HYBRID PERPETUAL GERANIUMS.—This class comprises but a limited number of varieties. their characteristics in most kinds being fragrance of leaves, with marked flowers, in the style of Pelargonium, but of smaller size. Flower more or less continually throughout the season.

SCENTED AND CUT-LEAVED GERANIUMS.—The Geranium family affords in this delightful section a remarkable diversity of sweet smelling odors in their foliage, resembling fruits, etc., which is not common with any other family of plants to anything like a similar extent. The *Rose, Apple, Lemon, Orange* and *Peppermint* are sufficiently distinct in fragrance that no imagination or fancy is required to detect the resemblance to the natural fruits, etc., from which they suggestively derive their names. The *Nutmeg* fragrance in the variety so called is not quite so apparent; neither is that of the *Citron* and *Pennyroyal*, yet these each possess quite a distinct fragrance which is agreeable and desirable for variety. The *Oak-leaved* variety resembles the oak leaf in shape; has clearly defined variegations and bears attractive pink flowers with brilliant dark spots on the petals. *Fernifolia* is a beautiful variety with very thin, finely cut leaves of fern-like texture and of a transparent green color, which renders it a real novelty. *Skeleton-leaved* is a very attractive variety with foliage of real skeleton-like appearance; that is to say, the leaves are singularly cut, the fleshy material lying along both sides of the framework ribs of the leaf, but generally less than *one-eighth of an inch* in width in any part. *Dr. Livingstone* somewhat resembles skeleton-leaved. *Lady Plymouth*, besides possessing fragrance, is similar in form of the foliage to the Rose, with distinct edges and variegations of white throughout. This is a beautiful variety for pot culture or for bedding out. *Shrubland Pet* is a free-growing variety with a sweet fragrance somewhat resembling Rose; it grows rapidly when bedded, assuming a height of eighteen inches, and bears constantly in summer hundreds of rich crimson flowers. *Little Pet* is a dwarf grower and profuse bloomer, with deep green foliage resembling the Rose in form; very desirable as a pot or summer bedding plant.

All the scented and cut-leaved Geraniums are valuable as pot plants, as they are not dependant upon bloom to make them attractive, although nearly all bear flowers freely, and some are really very desirable for their flowers alone. Their value as bedding plants seems not to be justly appreciated by cultivators. They are without exception rapid, handsome growers, and become in a short time after bedding exceedingly beautiful. All the varieties propagate readily from cuttings, except the Apple, which is reared from seed.

GESNERA ZEBRINA *(Greenhouse Bulbous Perennial, 35, 60, 90°).*

A pot plant with most beautiful velvety foliage, richly variegated in green and maroon. It dies down to the root at the approach of winter, after which water should be withheld almost entirely, keeping the pot in a warm place. In spring the bulb may be repotted, dividing it if desirable, and be given plenty of water to induce a new growth. Should have sandy loam soil, which will be the better for an admixture of thoroughly decayed leaf mould.

GLADIOLUS.

Of the summer flowering bulbs the Gladiolus stands eminently at the head, as the most imposing, varied and beautiful class. The flowers on a bed of good varieties are gorgeous and attractive beyond description. They are produced in spikes, two feet and upward in height, and have, especially the newer varieties, a rich, substantial texture, which make them the subjects of irresistible admiration from every one. By planting at intervals, from the middle of April to June, the flower garden may be brilliant with their colors for several months in summer and early autumn. Plant two or three inches deep and six or nine inches apart Keep tied to stakes, or, if in beds, to twine stretched across the bed. By the middle of October take up the bulbs, leave to dry for a few days, but not expose to frosts, remove the tops, and store in a moderately warm place for next year's planting. The rapid natural increase of the Gladiolus, under any common cultivation, together with the slight first cost of the bulbs, always tend to make the culture satisfactory.

Adonis, light cherry, marked with white. *Annatal Levanneur*, brilliant crimson, with maroon and azure. *Antonius*, cherry color, tinged with orange. *Aristole*, rosy lilac, mottled with crimson, yellow and carmine. *Berenice*, rose, streaked with carmine and purple. *Brenchleyensis*, deep vermillion scarlet; fine. *Chas. Dickens*, delicate rose, blazed with crimson rose. *Couranti Fulgens*, brilliant crimson, with yellow. *Daphne*, light cherry, with darker stripes, stained with carmine. *De Audry*, brilliant. *Don Juan*, rich fiery orange, with darker marks and blotches. *Emma*, clear deep carmine; dwarf. *Eugene Verdier*, rich carmine, with deep crimson spots. *Fanny Rouguet*, rosy flesh color, with carmine stripe; excellent. *Galathæa*, fine pinkish white, with carmine spots and stains. *Gandavensis*, red, marked with yellow, amaranth stripe. *Gem*, rosy lilac, slightly penciled with carmine and yellow. *Hercules*, fawn and scarlet, with yellow. *John Bull*, white, slightly tinged with lilac, and sometimes of pinkish color; large and excellent. *Lelia*, peach blossom, stained lilac. *Lord Byron*, brilliant scarlet, stained and ribboned pure white. *Madame de Vatry*, white, with violet crimson tint. *Madame Hercinque*, white, yellow, and rosy violet, marbled. *Madame Hocquin*, blotched and marbled scarlet. *Madame La Febre*, light pink and rose. *Madame Victor Verdier*, scarlet and rose, with violet spots. *Mars*, fine form and color. *Mazeppa*, rosy orange and red, large yellow stems; late. *Meteor*, dark brilliant red, with white stains. *Meyerbeer*, very brilliant light red, blazed with vermillion, amaranth stain; superb. *Mons. Vinchon*, light salmon red. *Nemesis*, rosy scarlet, with yellow and purple. *Ninon de Endor*, fine rose, flushed with carmine. *Osiris*, purplish rose, with dark blotches. *Pallas*, bright rose, shaded with orange. *Princess de Montrague*, brilliant red; dwarf. *Princess of Wales*, white, blazed with carminate rose. *Princess Fred. William*, flesh color, lightly streaked. *Proserpine*, rosy white, marked with deep rose and crimson. *Rembrandt*, bright scarlet. *Stuart Bow*, violet rose, stained deep rose. *Urania*, white, blazed with carminate rose. *Vesta*, white, shaded and marked with carmine pink. *Victoria*, rosy red, with a slight white center.

GNAPHALIUM LANATUM *(Greenhouse Perennial, 33, 45, 90°).*

A white foliaged plant, of spreading habit, about one foot high; well adapted for the front lines of ribbon beds, also fine for baskets and vases.

GODETIA *(Hardy Annual).*

Annuals of good quality, readily grown from seed, which may be sown where they are to flower. They will thrive in any garden soil, and will bloom nearly the entire season.

GOMPHRENA—ENGLISH CLOVER *(Half-Hardy Annual).*

An indispensable family of everlasting flowers, with colors as brilliant and showy as any belonging to this interesting class. Aside of the desirable quality in the flowers, of drying, and retaining their forms and colors for years, they are highly useful as summer decorative plants for planting singly in the border, or for massing and ribboning, on account of their attractive free-flowering habit; the flowers also being useful, in their fresh state, for summer cutting. The colors are white, flesh-color, dark purplish crimson, and orange. Sow the seed in a hot-bed or window-box, quite early, and transplant the young seedlings, the latter part of May, to a foot apart in the garden. By removing the cottony husk which envelopes the seed, it will germinate more freely. For drying, do not pick before they are of full size, which will be in August or September. Gomphrenas are also well adapted for pot culture in summer, flowering nearly as freely as in the open ground; for this purpose the soil should be rich, and no lack of water allowed.

GOLD DUST SHRUB—AUCUBA JAPONICA (*Greenhouse Perennial, 30, 45, 85°*).

A beautiful pot plant, prized for its attractive foliage; the leaves, which are large and smooth, are deep green and exquisitely blotched or speckled with golden yellow. The plant is almost hardy, and will thrive under the most ordinary culture; very desirable in the window, conservatory or for summer decoration in pots.

GRASSES FOR DRYING (*Annuals and Biennials*).

The varieties of these, though, of course, not brilliant, are interesting in the garden and desirable for cutting with flowers in summer; but they are particularly valuable to use with the everlasting flowers for the formation of winter bouquets, wreaths and other ornaments. For this purpose they should be cut in a green state and dried in the shade. *Agrostis Nebulosa*, most elegant ornamental grass; fine and feathery; very delicate. *Briza Maxima*, one of the best of the ornamental grasses; perfectly hardy; sow in the open ground any time in spring. *Briza Minor*, very small and pretty; sow early. *Bromus Brizæformis* is much like Briza Maxima, but is only useful the second summer after sowing. *Coix Lachryma* (Job's Tears), this grass is of no value for drying to be used in the formation of winter bouquets, but is grown for its wonderful bead-like seeds. These are hard as glass, possessing a glazed surface, and each seed is naturally punctured with a hole which admits of their being strung upon a thread, like beads. Not brilliant, but interesting and easily grown. *Langurus Ovatus* (Hare's Tail Grass), showy head; excellent. *Stipa Pennata* (Feather Grass), a most useful and exceedingly graceful and handsome grass for winter bouquets, flowering the second season. The rows should be distinctly labeled; the grass so nearly resembling ordinary grass that it would be in danger of being hoed out, unless guarded by some means.

GYMNOSTACHYUM (*Greenhouse Perennial, 38, 55, 90°*).

Beautiful pot plants for the conservatory or for Fernery culture in the window, with smooth leaves, richly painted with reticulations, in marks, which vary from red to rich pink on a deep green ground. A warm, damp, shady place suits them best.

GYPSOPHILA MURALIS (*Hardy Annual*).

A free flowering, graceful little plant for the garden. It is readily grown from the seed, and bears very small rose-colored flowers on many delicate stems, which gives to it an exceedingly light, airy appearance, somewhat resembling the seeds of some grasses.

HANGING BASKET, VASE AND TRELLIS PLANTS. Select list, page 18.

HELIANTHUS—SUN FLOWER (*Hardy Annual*).

A well known genus of rather coarse, large flowering plants for the garden, which can be rendered useful in mixed collections of tall growing Ricinus, Cannas, etc., in beds in the back ground. There are double and single varieties, all of which may be grown with the greatest ease by sowing the seed where they are to bloom.

HELICHRYSUM—EVERLASTING FLOWER (*Hardy Annual*).

Everlasting flowers of great merit for winter bouquets and other indoor decorations, as well as for their beauty in the flower garden in summer. There are several beautiful and even brilliant colors and shades, including dark purple, yellow, orange, white, bright rose, some of which are not common to the other families of everlastings, while with being very double they should not be overlooked by the cultivator who is seeking kinds suitable for drying. Cut the flowers before they are fully expanded, and also cure some of the buds, which make up beautifully, and are desirable for variety. The young plants transplant readily, and the seed may be sown in the hot-bed or in the house in April, setting the seedlings at a distance of a foot apart.

HELIOTROPE (*Greenhouse Perennial, 35, 50, 85°*).

An important plant either for pot culture in the winter or bedding out. The flowers, which are produced freely, are prized for their attractive light violet color—a color rare among choice flowers—but, above all, for the delicious vanilla-like scented odor emitted, which has given it a reputation above every other fragrant flowering plant that can be managed to produce bloom during the entire year. The plants make a rapid growth in the open air and bear an immense number of flowers until frost. For winter blooming in the window or conservatory it is best to start with young plants the spring previous, or some propagated from young shoots in June or July will do well and make large strong plants by the first of October, provided they have been brought along in rich soil; the plants never having become badly root-bound before they received a shift into larger pots; and always amply supplied with water. During winter give them the most sunny exposure that can be afforded, provided it is sufficiently warm, as they will not thrive in much shade. Wash the foliage occasionally and see that no red spider attacks the plants. The soil should contain a small portion of sand. The Heliotrope can be grown to a great age by training the shoots to a trellis, but I consider their culture more satisfactory, if the plants are renewed each year, keeping them bushy, by pinching back. There are numerous varieties in cultivation, but really so little difference exists between them that it is scarcely worth while to pay attention to procuring any but the best growing and most profuse blooming kinds. I have found the variety *Chieftain* to be a superior one for both summer and winter culture.

HELIPTERUM SANFORDII *(Tender Annual).*

A choice and distinct everlasting flower, growing less than one foot in height, with large globular clusters of bright golden yellow star-like flowers, which individually are of small size. Very desirable for winter bouquets, and cutting fresh in summer. Sow in heat and transplant to the garden after danger of frost is past.

HESPERIS MATRONALIS ALBA PLENO
(Hardy Herbaceous Perennial).

A fine hardy herbaceous plant, with spikes of clear white flowers a foot long, produced in early summer, which are highly esteemed for their fragrance and beauty.

HOLLYHOCK *(Hardy Herbaceous Perennial).*

A well known and splendid hardy plant for the garden, ranking with the Dahlia for autumn decoration, and, from its stately growth and the varied colors of its magnificent spikes of flowers, may justly demand a place in every collection where suitable situations for its tall growth are afforded. It may be perpetuated from the seed, or by dividing the roots. The plants flower the second year, from seed sown in the spring or before the first of September. To increase it by division, the stalks should be cut down in August, afterwards dividing the roots with a sharp knife. They are impatient of a wet soil and will winter badly unless grown where it is dry, a well drained light rich soil being best adapted for them.

HOYA CARNOSA—WAX PLANT *(Greenhouse Perennial, 35, 50, 90°).*

A house plant of climbing habit, that is also suitable for conservatory culture, with finely formed, thick, waxy foliage. The flowers, which are produced in clusters, have a pearly, wax-like appearance, are star-shaped, with a pink or crimson center. They are of easy culture and continue to increase in beauty for years; should be provided with a suitable trellis for support. The Hoya does not require much water, and, when growing in the window, should have its foliage cleaned of accumulating dust occasionally.

HYACINTH *(Hardy Bulb).*

The Hyacinth is a well-known family of those hardy bulbs that are planted in the fall and which flower early in the spring. In common with the Tulip, Crocus, etc., it is adapted for winter flowering in the window or conservatory, and is preferred above all other bulbs for such purposes. The flowers are very fragrant, of beautiful form, both double and single, possess attractive colors, and remain beautiful for a great length of time, either when forced or in the open air. In the garden they should be planted six or eight inches apart and four inches deep. On pages 14 and 21 will be found directions for cultivating the Hyacinth, and other bulbs of similar requirements, in the garden and in pots for winter blooming.

Fig. 47. Double Hollyhock.

HYDRANGEA *(Greenhouse Perennial, 32, 45, 80°).*

Hydrangea Hortensis is a well-known pot plant, and much esteemed for its great profusion of elegant but monstrous flowers, which pass in rotation through several shades of pink colors, and remain upon the plant for months. The plants succeed much better in a shady place than where it is sunny, on which account they are valuable for house culture. It requires a plentiful supply of water during its growth, and especially when in flower—the flowers being produced upon shoots of the previous year. Being tolerably hardy, in the Southern States it may be planted in the open air and remain out during winter with protection, and will flower profusely from June to October. *H. Hortensis Variegata* is a somewhat rare and beautiful variety of the preceding, with the foliage distinctly blotched with clear white upon green. It is readily grown and forms one of the most delightful variegated house plants which can be cultivated.

ICE PLANT.   See Mesembryanthemum.

IBERIS.   See Candytuft.

IPOMŒA *(Tender Annual).*

A splendid family of climbers, with which the Morning Glory, as *Ipomœa purpurea*, is classed by some, although all the varieties, besides, are more tender than this well-known, useful climber. Our seasons are rather short in the North to derive great satisfaction from the tender kinds, unless they are brought forward in heat. By sowing the seed in March or April and cultivating in pots, or transplanting, with great care, to a sheltered situation in the ground after June first, they will amply repay all the care bestowed upon them, and will, by this means, flower profusely and until frosts. There will be little use of sowing the seeds in the open ground before the last of May, as the soil must be warm to enable them to germinate. The seeds are hard, and previous to sowing should be soaked in boiling water, and allowed to remain until the water is cold. The Ipomœas are very desirable plants for cultivation in pots for conservatory decoration. Under any circumstances, they require a soil well enriched with rotten manure.

I. Coccinea (Star Ipomœa), a handsome variety of free growth and profuse blooming habit, especially after midsummer. Small, bright scarlet flowers that are very attractive. Does quite well, ordinarily, by sowing in the open ground, towards the end of May. *I. Hederacea grandiflora* includes several beautiful varieties, with flowers somewhat similar to the Morning Glory, but much larger and of the most delicate colors, such as light blue, blue with a white edge, blue with a purple center, white with pink center, and white shaded with purplish red. They are exceedingly handsome and well repay the care necessary to rear them. *I. Quamoclit* (Cypress Vine), an exceedingly beautiful variety that, for elegance of foliage, gracefulness of habit, and loveliness of flowers, is without a rival among annual climbing plants, although it is quite tender. There are scarlet, white and rose-colored flowers, which open in the morning, and contrast delightfully with the rich green, delicate cut foliage.

IRIS—FLOWER DE LUCE *(Hardy Perennial Bulbs and Tubers).*

Garden plants of elegant habit and beautiful flowers, comprising several divisions—those most commonly met with being the *English* and *Spanish Iris*, which are bulbous, and the *German Iris*, well-known hardy, tuberous perennials, generally known by the name of Flag Lily, and which thrive in any garden soil.

ENGLISH AND SPANISH IRIS.—This division includes numerous varieties, flowering in June, which embrace the most delicate shades of light and dark blue, brown, purple, yellow, white, and variously striped and spotted flowers of exceedingly handsome appearance. The bulbs should be planted in autumn, with Hyacinths, Tulips and other hardy bulbs (see directions, page 14), and need not be taken up oftener than once in three years. Are also desirable for pot culture in winter (see "Culture of Hyacinths and other Hardy Bulbs for Winter Decoration," page 21). The English varieties are of more robust growth than the Spanish, but in other respects quite similar.

GERMAN IRIS.—These are valuable plants for the garden, being of the easiest culture in any soil, and produce many beautiful flowers in the spring. There are numerous varieties, of various colors and shades of yellow, blue, purple, white and salmon—some distinctly of one color, and others striped, spotted and tipped with various colors. The tubers grow rapidly and should be taken up once every three or four years, and be reset.

IVY—HEDERA *(Hardy and Tender Perennials).*

I take pleasure in introducing a full page plate of Ivy foliage, considerably reduced in size, upon which are represented some of the most distinct and interesting varieties of this useful family of plants. Sometimes I think the reason why Ivies are not grown in every home is, because amateurs have not all seen or became acquainted with their admirable adaptability to house culture. In the first place the Ivy *naturally* delights in a situation partially or wholly shaded from the sun, which allows of its growing or being trained—for it is climbing in habit —in any part of the room, and at a distance from the window; then again, wholly unlike many plants, it is not at all particular as regards temperature, or if the atmosphere be dry or damp; frosts do not affect it, as it is evergreen, and all the varieties are nearly, some quite, hardy in the latitude of Buffalo, and, on the other hand, it bears 75° or upwards of heat with impunity. The plant requires but little attention, is exceptionally free of insects and

Fig. 48. Group of Ivy Leaves.

1. *Hedera Gracilis.*
2. *H. Marginata Elegantissima.*
3. *H. Marginata Cullissi.*
4. *H. Carariensis* (English Ivy).
5. *H. Latifolia Maculata.*
6. *H. Chrysocarpa.*

7. *Hedera Japonica Argentea.*
8. *H. Rhomba Variegata.*
9. *H. Folia Picta.*
10. *H. Palmata* (Palm-leaf Ivy).
11. *H. Bicolor.*
12. *H. Poetica* (Poet's Ivy).

would continue to thrive for a long time under neglect that would kill most other plants outright. It is true the Ivy ordinarily bears no flowers, but the foliage presents a remarkably bright, clean, glossy appearance, and is of an attractive deep green color, except where variegated or blotched; besides in the different varieties numerous distinct and interesting forms and variegations exist permanently, that we do not mind the lack in this respect. The Ivy is very tractable, and if planted in a large-sized pot and permanently placed in the parlor or sitting room, it may be trained to cover the side of the room or ceiling, festoon a pillar, climb and trail about a windowsill, or up a wire screen or trellis, and endless other uses. Fig. 49 represents a plant used to decorate a picture or mirror frame. In planting for this delightful purpose no earthen pot is used, but instead, the plant is grown in a wedge-shaped zinc pot or pan, open at the top, placed behind the frame. It is also unequaled as a climber or drooper for hanging baskets. As a rule, the variegated varieties are of slower growth than the others and not so good for planting where a large space is to be covered with foliage, but for pot culture they are unequaled. Propagate easily from cuttings or by layers.

Fig. 49. Ivy Trained about Frame.

H. Bicolor, a variety of free growth, edged silvery white (No. 11 on plate). *H. Canariensis* (English Ivy), an excellent variety for cultivation in the house, being a free grower, and very beautiful (No. 4 on plate). *H. Canariensis Marmarata*, very similar to the above, except that the foliage is distinctly marbled with silvery white and yellow; vigorous. *H. Chrysocarpa*, exceedingly pretty, narrow elongated leaves; a handsome and free grower (No. 6 on plate). *H. Folio Picta*, leaves clearly blotched with golden yellow (No. 9 on plate). *H. Gracilis*, a slender, rapid growing variety, with attractive narrow lobed leaves; by pinching back the ends of shoots, to induce a dense growth, it forms a beautiful pot plant without a trellis; also superior as a drooper in baskets, vases, etc., (No. 1 on plate). *H. Helix* (Irish Ivy) the hardiest of all Ivies, leaf similar to Canariensis; will thrive unprotected in the North, if planted where the sun in winter cannot strike it. *H. Japonica Argentea*, silver-margined Japanese, distinct (No. 7 on plate). *H. Latifolia Maculata*, a free growing variety, marbled and blotched in a very attractive manner (No. 5 on plate). *H. Marginata Cullissi*, Cullis' silver-margined, very fine (No. 3 on plate). *H. Marginata Elegantissima*, margined with light yellow (No. 2 on plate). *H. Palmata* (Palm-leaf Ivy), an attractive and interesting Ivy, with beautifully defined foliage (No. 10 on plate). *H. Poetica* (Poet's Ivy), a handsome variety, of beautiful form of leaf and growth (No. 12 on plate). *H. Regneriana*, very large leaves of roundish outline and massive growth. *H. Rhomba variegata*, silver margined, distinct and beautiful (No. 8 on plate).

JAPANESE STRIPED MAIZE *(Tender Annual).*

A plant closely allied and quite similar to the common Indian Corn, the foliage of which is beautifully and freely striped throughout its entire length with white of various widths, rendering the plant'very effective when grouped with Cannas, Helianthus, Hollyhocks, Ricinus, etc., or if planted in ribbon lines. May be started in pots about May 1st, or planted where wanted several weeks later. The plant retains its attractiveness for a long time, as it does not tassel and seed as freely as the common Maize or Indian Corn.

JASMINUM GRANDIFLORUM *(Greenhouse Perennial, 35, 50 to 60, 85°).*

A plant for pot culture, of climbing habit, with delicately cut foliage, and which is esteemed for the fragrance of its pure white single flowers. Fine for winter flowering in a warm light window or in the conservatory; it can be trained to a stake or trellis, or be planted for twining up the pillars of the latter. The soil in which it is grown should be loose and of a fertile character. Propagates with some difficulty from cuttings.

JONQUIL. See Narcissus.

JUSTICA CARNEA *(Greenhouse Perennial, 35, 50, 90°).*

An upright growing pot plant of free growth, crowned with rosy pink spikes of flowers nearly the whole year. They are easily cultivated in any soil, but it should be well drained with pot shreds or gravel, and be given abundant pot room.

LADY'S EAR DROP. See Fuchsia.

LANTANA *(Greenhouse Perennial, 35, 50, 90°).*

These desirable plants are annually growing in favor, both for bedding purposes and pot culture. They are of brilliant colors, robust growth, and profuse blooming habits, which render them worthy of a place in every considerable collection. The flowers have somewhat the appearance of Verbenas, but are grown on shrub-like plants, and are of the most delicate shades of orange, sulphur, creamy white, etc., which colors are not found in that plant. Also interesting from the fact of their changing from one distinct color to another on the same plant, as they increase in development and age. In the house they should be placed in a light warm place; are particularly useful for window culture, as they will thrive in a dryer atmosphere than many plants. By proper pruning, plants may be grown of handsome shape. Somewhat difficult to propagate.

LAVENDULA CRISTATA *(Greenhouse Perennial, 33, 45, 90°).*

A neat, compact, pot and bedding plant, useful in baskets, vases, etc., and of the easiest culture. The leaves are of an ashy green, an inch long, nearly round, of singular notched appearance, seeming to have been shaped in a mould. Propagates from cuttings.

LARKSPUR. See Delphinium.

LAURUSTINUS *(Greenhouse Perennial, 33, 50, 90°).*

A shrubby perennial for pot culture, that blooms freely only in winter and early spring. The flowers are pure white, produced in large flattened panicles, and are universally esteemed. The foliage is deep green, smooth and of pretty form. It is quite hardy, and in the South will stand the winters with slight protection. The plant always assumes a handsome form, and is seldom troubled with insects. In summer the pots should be moved to the open air and plunged.

LEMON. See Orange and Lemon.

LEMON VERBENA. See Aloysia Citriodora.

LEPTOSIPHON *(Hardy Annual).*

A charming class of free blooming annuals of the easiest culture from seed. They are of bushy growth and produce an abundance of small flowers of remarkably distinct colors. Sow the seed where they are to bloom early in the spring, or it may be done the fall previous.

L. Aureus is less than six inches high and spreads to the width of one foot. Very handsome as an edging plant, being covered with a profusion of exceedingly pretty, little yellow flowers with dark centre, which gives them a peculiar rich appearance. *L. Densiflorus Albus,* one foot high, pure white; very useful for loose bouquets. There is also a rosy lilac variety similar to this, but being of less desirable color is not so greatly esteemed. *L. Hybridus,* French hybrids of pretty appearance, which embrace yellow, orange, rose, purple and other colors.

LIBONIA FLORIBUNDA *(Greenhouse Perennial, 32, 45 or 50, 85°).*

A neat growing, winter blooming plant well adapted for the window shelf or conservatory. The flowers, which are about an inch in length, are scarlet orange at the base, running into deep yellow at the top, somewhat similar to the Cigar flower, but larger. They are produced freely under ordinary circumstances, and are quite certain of affording pleasure to the cultivator. The plants are of the easiest culture, any well enriched soil suiting them. A frost among plants of sufficient severity to injure many, would leave this unharmed.

LILIUM—LILY *(Hardy Perennial Bulb).*

The Lilium family, including the numerous superb varieties from Japan, are eminently valuable garden plants, and no collection can scarcely be so limited but that some of the choicer varieties at least should be included. They possess many desirable qualities, being, with an exception or two, perfectly hardy; easy of culture in any dry soil, continuing to increase in strength and beauty for many years, and, above all, are of matchless colors in the several varieties. *L. Longiflorum* is the principal exception to their being entirely hardy, and this will stand the winter well, with a protection of strawy manure on the roots, applied late in the fall after the ground is frozen. Such a covering is desirable for all the varieties, and especially newly planted ones. Lilies may be planted either in the fall months, or early in the spring. Avoid applying rank manure to the soil, which is apt to cause a diseased condition in the bulbs. They should be set deep, the top of the bulbs not less than four inches below the surface. This is essential, in order that the roots which support the flowering shoot, and which being *above* the bulb, may be fully protected from the sun in summer. They should be allowed to remain several years without resetting, if possible. The various Lilies can also be cultivated to a great degree of perfection in pots, with ordinary care.

L. Atrosanguineum, orange red, blotched and marbled. *L. Auratum* (Golden Banded Japan Lily), this Lily is of remarkable size and magnificence, usually measuring nearly a foot across. It is delicately fragrant, and is composed of six petals of ivory whiteness, each thickly studded with crimson spots, and having a golden band lengthwise through its centre. Will succeed in any dry deep soil, but cannot be considered quite as robust as most other varieties, yet

5

is not very delicate. *L. Candidum*, the ordinary fragrant White Lily, frequently found in cultivation. It flowers about the first of July on stems three or four feet high, and a mass of the plants are always beheld with admiration. There is a double flowering variety of this sort, which, however, will not compare with the single in point of desirability. *L. Lancifolium Album, Roseum*, and *Rubrum* are introductions from Japan, of the very highest merit for garden culture. The three varieties are quite similar in form, but vary in color—the former being pure white of great purity and beauty, but the plant is a little delicate in character. The two latter varieties are almost alike in appearance, being of ivory white ground, spotted in rose and red, and quite fragrant. They are very hardy, and flower in August, strong plants producing numerous flowers on stalks three feet high. *L. Longiflorum*, snowy white, trumpet-shaped flowers, five inches in length. Although a vigorous variety, it should be treated as not being quite hardy. This variety is suitable for forcing to flower in winter in the window or conservatory. *L. Tigrinum* (Tiger Lily), a well known strong growing variety, the flowers of which are orange spotted with black. A new variety of this desirable old sort has recently been introduced, having excellent double flowers. *L. Washingtonianum*, a recent introduction from the Far West, California and Oregon. It produces delicately fragrant, pendulous flowers which are pure white shaded with lilac.

Fig. 50. Pansies. See page 71.

LILY OF THE VALLEY—Convallaria Majallis *(Hardy Perennial).*

For a combination of elegance, purity, grace and fragrance in a small compass, this little flower is without a just rival in the garden, and it has been esteemed as a favorite for ages. The flowers are pure white, bell-shaped, and less than one-third of an inch across. They droop gracefully, each on its own curved stem, from the side of an upright stem six, and upwards, inches long, supporting a dozen or more of the flowers. The leaves, which spring from the root, are, in themselves, most elegant, being large and smooth, of a luxuriant green, and furnish an admirable accompaniment to the flowers in choice floral arrangements. Flowers may be forced quite readily in the window and conservatory, by taking up and potting clumps in the fall, and after subjecting them to several severe freezes, bringing them into a heat of forty-five or fifty degrees, in the night time, and giving an abundance of water. In our great cities much attention is paid to forcing this plant in winter as the flowers are eagerly sought, at remunerative prices, by lovers of choice flowers all during the winter months. The plants are perfectly hardy and will succeed well in a shady place, in any garden soil, flowering in May and June. They increase rapidly by their slender roots, which spread to a considerable distance. Altogether may be considered one of the most desirable plants in cultivation.

LOBELIA *(Greenhouse and Hardy Perennials, 32, 45, 80°).*

The Lobelias are universally admired, and the drooping varieties are used to an extent, probably, second to no other plant in cultivation, for planting in hanging baskets and similar arrangements for decoration. Their graceful, drooping and free blooming habit renders them especially valuable for such purposes, as, under favorable circumstances, the flowers are produced by hundreds for a long time. They are equally desirable as pot plants, forming a dense mass of drooping foliage and flowers over the edge of the pot, in a most pleasing manner. Among our most suitable plants for window culture, as they flower almost constantly and equally as well in shady places, as in the full sun, while their delight in an abundance of moisture in the soil, is easily afforded them. When bedded out they flower during the entire season, so profusely, as to render them very useful, for ribboning or massing, where low growing plants are desired. This is especially the case in a wet season, or if the soil is frequently watered. Propagate freely from cuttings.

L. Cardinalis (Cardinal Flower), a splendid, hardy native plant, of excellent upright habit; producing spikes of brilliant scarlet flowers, of a dazzling hue; excellent either for pot culture or for bedding. *L. Erinus grandis*, large blue; in every way excellent as a drooper for hanging baskets, vases, etc., or for pot culture. *L. Erinus Paxtonia*, similar to the preceding, but is blue, with a white eye. *L. Miss Murphy*, a neat dwarf grower; very beautiful, either as a pot plant or for planting in beds and borders. It grows a dense globular tuft, six inches in diameter, and can be trimmed to any desired shape.

LUPINUS—LUPINE *(Hardy Annual).*

A genus of annuals for the garden that are rather showy, and flower until after hard frosts; in fact the beds will frequently appear at their best late in October and November, after the larger proportion of summer flowers are past their usefulness. Blue, white and purple are the principal colors, being distinct in some varieties and intermixed with yellow in others. The seed should be sown early where they are to bloom.

LYCHNIS *(Hardy Perennial).*

A useful family of hardy garden and pot plants, of easy culture and free bloomers, which are throughout, exceedingly showy of flowers. Some of the varieties are easily grown from seed, flowering the first season if sown early; others propagate by division of the roots, and still others with difficulty from cuttings. They delight in a light rich soil.

L. Chalcedonica, a tall kind, growing two feet in height, which produces in the variety most generally cultivated, heads of intense light scarlet flowers, and in others white and flesh-colored flowers respectively. May be propagated from seed or by dividing the roots early in the spring of alternate years; succeeds best if protected during winter. *L. Fimbriata*, double pink flowers on stalks a foot high; very showy and desirable and perfectly hardy. *L. Flos Cuculi Flore albo pleno* (Double White Lychnis), a valuable summer bloomer; in flower from the middle of June until October; flowers pure white, somewhat resembling a Carnation; very highly esteemed by cultivators. Should be protected by a covering of straw or leaves at the opening of winter. *L. Flos Cuculi pleno* (Ragged Robin), well known hardy plants, flowering in May. The flowers are crimson and double. *L. Fulgens* is a hardy species with scarlet flowers; one and one-half feet high. *L. Haageana*, of dwarfish growth about one foot high, readily raised from seed. The flowers are large, single and embrace white, rose, red and vermillion-colored varieties.

LYCOPODIUM—SELAGINELLA *(Greenhouse Perennial, 35, 55, 90°).*

Delicate fine foliage plants of creeping and erect habits, that delight in warm, moist, partially shaded situations, being, with the Ferns, an unequaled class of plants for Fernery culture. Properly treated they are a delight to every cultivator, no matter what may be the extent of his or her collection.

LYTHRUM SALICARIA *(Hardy Herbaceous Perennial).*

A hardy garden plant, growing to the height of three feet and producing long attractive spikes of rosy-red flowers through the season. Propagates by dividing the roots.

MARIGOLD—TAGETES *(Half-Hardy Annual).*

Well known free flowering annuals, with single and double, also quilled varieties, of sulphur, orange, brown and striped flowers. They are reared with the greatest ease from seed sown either in heat or where they are to flower. Although there are some exceedingly rich and showy varieties, which are attractive wherever employed, yet the plants will never be ranked among the highest by cultivators, on account of their rather distasteful fragrance, but are decidely too beautiful to be entirely ignored for this reason.

TAGETES SIGNATA PUMILIA.—A splendid half-hardy annual, forming a dense globular mass from one to one and one-half feet in diameter, and producing hundreds of bright yellow and orange flowers on the surface. It is a handsome plant for the garden, and as easily grown from seed as are the common Marigolds.

MESEMBRYANTHEMUM, INCLUDING ICE AND DEW PLANTS *(Greenhouse Perennial, 33, 45 to 60, 90°).*

A genus for the most part natives of the Cape of Good Hope. There are many varieties, but the several I will here notice are the most valuable for ordinary cultivation, and are highly prized wherever introduced. All of these are of trailing habit, and being free growers they are consequently very desirable for planting in baskets, vases, etc. They are also excellent for pot culture in the window or conservatory, and very handsome if bedded, continuing in flower during most of the season, and growing with great freedom in rich ground.

M. Chrystallinium (Ice Plant), this variety is noted for the peculiar cold, icy appearance the foliage presents, the stems and leaves throughout being covered with crystal frost-like gems, which render the plant very attractive. Grown from seed, and should be treated as a tender annual. *M. Cordifolium* (Dew Plant), another variety possessing the remarkable features of the Ice Plant to a slight extent, but, aside of this, is a stronger and more handsome grower generally, with rich deep green foliage, and is covered with a profusion of attractive small rosy-pink blossoms almost constantly. This is one of the handsomest, drooping plants in cultivation for hanging baskets, vases, etc., and also as a low, trailing bedding plant. Propagates from cuttings. *M. Cordifolium variegatum,* similar to the preceding, but in addition, the foliage is variegated in creamy white and green, which renders it exceedingly pretty for any use it is suited to. *M. Grandiflorum,* a variety with round-pointed foliage, producing large pink flowers several inches in diameter, more or less continually from early spring throughout the season.

MIGNONETTE—RESEDA *(Hardy Annual).*

A deliciously fragrant flower, two well known to require any special description. It is easily grown from seed, which may be sown very early in the spring where they are to flower, and several times during the season for an abundance in succession, and may also be sown late in the fall. Every garden should have a bed for cutting from. Some pots may be started in summer for winter flowering in the window or conservatory. Do not transplant well.

MIMOSA SENSITIVA—SENSITIVE PLANT *(Tender Annual).*

A remarkable annual cultivated for the curious peculiarity of its delicate pinnate leaves, which suddenly close and droop if touched or shaken. They open and regain their upright position in the course of an hour or two, without the least injury to themselves or the plant for the surprising transition through which they have passed. The plant is only suitable for pot culture, and may easily be reared from seed by sowing in a warm window or hot-bed.

MIRABILIS JALAPA—FOUR O'CLOCK FLOWER *(Half-Hardy Annual or Perennial),*

A very ornamental plant of good habit; glossy bright foliage with fragrant flowers, which open about four o'clock in the afternoon, hence its appropriate common name. The plant grows to several feet in height, and blooms profusely after mid-summer. The flowers include various colors, such as different shades of red, red striped with white, red and yellow, yellow, lilac striped with white, violet and white, and sport into many attractive variegations. May be reared from seed planted in May where the plants are desired, or the roots may be taken up in the fall and preserved like Dahlias during winter. The plants should stand two feet apart.

M. Jalapa folis variegata, a variety of the above, the leaves of which are faintly variegated or marbled; several colors of flowers. *M. Longiflora alba* and *violacea,* with long, sweet scented flowers, in the former, pure white with purple below, and in the latter, violet.

MORNING GLORY. See Convolvulus.

MUSK PLANT. See description of Mimulus Moschatus, page 18.

MYOSOTIS—FORGET-ME-NOT *(Half-Hardy Perennial).*

An old and well known genus of garden plants, growing about six inches high, which survive our winters with protection. They bear in different varieties blue, yellow and white star-like flowers with bright centers; very small, but highly esteemed for their distinctness and perfection of form; these appear in little clusters during the greater portion of the season, if the plants are grown in moist soil in a somewhat shaded situation—a condition most favorable to their growth. Easily raised from seed sown in early spring or in August.

MYRTUS COMMUNIS—MYRTLE *(Greenhouse Perennial, 32, 45 to 50, 90°).*

This, the true Myrtle, is a pretty pot plant of erect shrubby habit, which has been grown and highly esteemed for ages very remote. At the present day it is valued by florists for its twigs of small dark, smooth foliage, which are a useful green in making wedding and funeral bouquets and designs of white flowers, besides being slightly fragrant. The plant bears small white flowers quite freely, and is of the easiest culture in the window or conservatory.

MYRSYPHYLLUM ASPARAGOIDES—SMILAX *(Greenhouse Perennial, 33, 45 to 55, 90°)*.

One of the finest climbing plants in existence, for pot culture, hanging baskets, etc., being esteemed for the exceeding grace and delicacy of the vine and its beautiful glossy green foliage.

Fig. 51. Smilax (Myrsyphyullum Asparagoides).

Smilax has become conspicuous among plants cultivated by florists for foliage alone, and large beds are now devoted, summer and winter, to cultivating a supply. Each plant is provided with a twine for support, which extends upward to the rafters or sash bars of greenhouses, and upon which the numerous shoots twine. After the top has been reached, the entire length is cut away for use, and another twine is fixed, which in turn answers for a support for the new shoots that quickly start again from the root. The stems of foliage are usually sold by the yard, and are greatly in demand for festooning, and for cutting into short lengths to intermix with arrangements of choice flowers. For window cultivation the plants should be trained to strings or trellis, and be kept near the glass. Smilax is closely allied to common garden Asparagus, and like that plant will bear frequent cutting back to the roots. After a large growth has been obtained, the plant should be entirely cut away as soon as the leaves are inclined to turn yellow; the root should then be given a rest for a month or two by withholding water almost wholly, after which it may be started into a new growth. Will thrive in any soil; is propagated from seed.

NARCISSUS *(Hardy Bulb)*.

An early spring flowering bulbous family, which embrace numerous forms and colors of flowers, including the well known Daffodil and Jonquil. The flowers appear very early, and are highly ornamental. Nearly all are hardy, and should be planted in the autumn like the Hyacinth, etc., but should remain in the ground until they form large clumps, when they may be divided and reset. All the kinds are desirable, and some are unequaled for pot culture in winter in the window and conservatory (see " Culture of Hardy Bulbs for Winter Decoration," page 21):

DOUBLE NARCISSUS (Daffodil, etc.), include besides the double yellow Daffodil, varieties of white (Albo pleno odorata; very handsome), light yellow, orange and other colors, all of which are double, and some deliciously fragrant. Very hardy and desirable in every garden, also useful for forcing.

SINGLE NARCISSUS are hardy and of great beauty, including *N. Poeticus* (Poet's Narcissus), a snowy white variety, in which the projecting cup from the centre is of cream color, delicately fringed with reddish purple. *N. Bulbocodium* (Hoop-Petticoat Narcissus), having the cup two inches long, and broad at the brim. *N. Odorus* (known as Great Jonquil), a large yellow variety with powerful fragrance; and other desirable varieties.

POLYANTHUS NARCISSUS, an exceedingly handsome division, but not sufficiently hardy in the North to be reliable in the open ground. They will sometimes succeed if planted deep in light, dry soil and heavily protected at the approach of winter. It is in pot culture in winter, however, either in the window or conservatory, that this species can be employed with the greatest advantage by cultivators, and for this purpose nothing can be more satisfactory. There are numerous varieties, which show many colors and shades, from purest white to orange red. The flowers appear in clusters, numbering from six to upwards of a dozen on each. The white flowers of this division have yellow cups, and the yellow, orange cups. There is also a double variety which is very fragrant.

NARCISSUS JONQUILLA (Jonquil).—The Jonquils are well known hardy bulbs, producing both double and single sweet scented flowers which are very attractive. Plant in autumn six inches apart and cover three inches deep. They do not flower so well the first year as the second and third, therefore should only be lifted every third year.

NASTURTIUM. See Tropæolum.

NEMOPHILA *(Hardy Annual).*

A genus of low growing annuals which afford in the different varieties many peculiar and novel colored flowers, such as white with black spots, white and purple, white blotched with violet, white with chocolate centre, black edged with white, rich maroon margined white, bright blue with white centre, blue blotched with black, and so forth. While interesting, these plants can scarcely be styled showy, although when at their best they are very attractive. A cool partially shaded situation suits them best. The seeds should be sown in frames early in the spring or late the fall previous, in order to secure strong plants by hot weather, as young plants that come on late, never do so well. Transplant to five or six inches apart.

NIREMBERGIA GRANDIFLORA *(Greenhouse Perennial, 33, 45, 90°).*

A valuable plant, either for the flower garden, or in baskets, pots, vases, window boxes, etc. The leaves are small and pointed, flowers pale bluish white, one inch and a half in diameter and salver shaped. They are borne in great abundance all during the summer, and by fall fifty flowers can, almost at any time, be counted on each plant that is growing in the garden. They may be lifted in October without wilting, and will be showy for a long time in the window or conservatory. Any soil will suit them. Propagate from cuttings with some difficulty.

OLEANDER—NERIUM *(Greenhouse Perennial, 30, 45, 85°)*

A well known genus of erect growing, evergreen shrubs, with narrow elongated leathery leaves. The plants are well adapted for culture in pots and boxes, for adorning the lawn, or plant collection in summer, as they are easily managed to produce an abundance of bloom. They naturally delight in moist soil, and during their flowering season should at all times be well supplied with water. After they have done blooming, keep rather dry at the roots until spring, storing them during winter in any cool dry place, a light cellar answering very well. Early winter is the most suitable time for pruning the plants, which may be done quite severely to their benefit. The young shoots can be cut back to within two buds of the old wood. In March they should be shifted into larger pots or boxes and a new growth encouraged by an increase of water. Decayed turfy loam, with one-fourth part old rotten manure, forms an excellent compost for them. As the plants advance in growth, a weekly watering of liquid manure, not very strong, will heighten the size and beauty of the flowers ; during their approaching season of bloom, keep a sharp look-out for scale insects on the leaves and bark and remove them by washing. Scrubbing affected parts with tobacco water heated to 100° and afterwards with soap and water will completely destroy them if it is thoroughly done. The Oleander is easily propagated from cuttings of the young growth in spring and summer. A favorite and time-honored method of proceeding with this, is by placing the cutting in a bottle of water suspended in the window or under the piazza; this means is quite similar to the saucer system of propagation described on page 16, and in the case of this plant is perhaps quite as good a one. Immediately as the roots appear, the cutting should be potted and receive an abundance of water until it becomes rooted in the soil.

Alba Plena is a semi-double pure white variety, not so commonly cultivated as Splendens, but nevertheless very desirable. *Splendens* is a very beautiful variety with double, rose colored flowers, which render it highly esteemed by all cultivators. *Yellow,* a single pale yellow variety, which is useful for affording a greater diversity of colors.

ORANGE AND LEMON—CITRUS *(Greenhouse Perennials, 32, 45 to 55, 90°).*

These well known fruits of commerce both belong to the genus *Citrus,* and are quite identical in many respects. The genus comprises a great number of kinds and varieties, some of which are known as wild and others as cultivated, the former possessing little value, except as stocks upon which to graft the better sorts. Both the Orange and Lemon can easily be cultivated in pots in the North, and form attractive plants when in health with their rich glossy leaves which are also pleasantly fragrant if chafed. Under favorable circumstances they may be had to flower and fruit in the window or conservatory, and if the stocks be grafted with the improved varieties the fruit produced will be edible, although such varieties are always more difficult to cultivate than the stronger growing plants produced from seed. The flowers of the Orange are noted for their sweetness and pure white color in some of the kinds. There are beautiful dwarf growing varieties of the Orange, which are known as the *Chinese Dwarf,* that are very suitable for cultivation, being of good habit and producing fruit freely, which, although not edible, renders the plant highly ornamental. These can be perpetuated by cuttings, thus allowing of their purity being maintained to any extent. The genus loves a rich soil, and one containing a fair proportion of well decayed turf, taken up from a loamy soil, will suit it as well as any. For young plants, it may contain a portion of sand until they arrive at a fruiting age. The months of March, and also August, are suitable times for repotting the plants, which may also be pruned at the same time. All stunted or straggling shoots should be well cut back and a general system of pruning be adopted to effect a well shaped head. The Lemon especially, is greatly inclined to irregularity of growth. All the varieties of the Citrus tribe are shade-loving plants, and should, therefore, be protected from the full glare of sunshine in midsummer, but throughout winter they should have all the daylight that can be secured for them. The foliage and branches should also receive an occasional cleansing with water and sponge, and insects of no kind must be tolerated.

PÆONIA *(Hardy Herbaceous Perennial).*

A well known genus of plants noted for their hardiness, ease of culture, vigorous growth in any garden soil, and for the wonderful size and attractiveness of their flowers, which in many varieties are nearly half a foot in diameter, well rounded and perfectly double. The Herbaceous Pæonias are increased by dividing the roots. This may be done once every few years, in September or October or in the spring, if it be done very early. The roots should be taken up whole, cut in pieces, each with at least one bud, and be reset. Plant them in rich deep soil, the crown or bud three inches below the surface.

PANICUM *(Hardy Herbaceous and Greenhouse Perennials).*

PANICUM PLICATUM.—This is a desirable hardy grass for the garden, with deep green foliage, striped white, and occasionally rose ; grows in clumps, and attains a height of about two feet ; propagates by division. Protect in winter.

PANICUM VARIEGATUM *(35, 50 to 60, 90°).*—A very attractive grass, of trailing or creeping habit, excellent for hanging baskets or pot culture in the greenhouse or window. The leaves are willow shaped, and distinctly variegated with white, rose and green. The plant requires a warm place, and rather delights in shade ; propagates from cuttings.

PANSY—HEART'S-EASE, VIOLA TRICOLOR *(Hardy Annual).* See Fig. 50.

I term the Pansy a hardy annual because the best way to manage the plants is to treat them as such, although they may not incorrectly be classed among biennials and perennials. The Pansy is a magnificent genus among flowering plants, and is undoubtedly as generally esteemed as any in cultivation, not even excepting the Rose. It is among the easiest to rear from the seed; is very productive of flowers for a long time, and the flowers in the garden are the subjects of admiration from all beholders. Their colors range from white to jet black through the various shades of violet, dark and light blue, red, bronze, yellow, purple, etc., and there are some varieties of recent introduction which are most beautifully and distinctly striped and blotched. To grow the Pansy to perfection simply requires that they be planted in soil of high fertility, and with this requisite secured there is no need of hot-bed, conservatory, or any other appliance to have an abundance of flowers, by sowing the seed in the fall. They flower most freely, and the bloom is finest in the months preceding and following the hottest and dryest part of summer, although there will be no cessation of bloom during this period if the soil is ordinarily retentive of moisture and well enriched. The seeds may be sown in August or the first half of September. If the seed-bed is shaded with whitewashed sash or lath shutters—the lath an inch apart—they will germinate more readily. After they have made their second leaves they should be thinned out to afford a chance for development, or they may be transplanted to several inches apart in any rich soil for wintering. Young Pansy plants are hardy, and all the protection they require is a *slight* scattering of long strawy manure on the beds, after the ground is frozen, which will prevent any injury to the plants from thawing weather in winter; this must be removed early in the spring. For final flowering, plant six to nine inches apart in the highly enriched beds above alluded to. If the sowing in the fall was neglected, the seed may be sown from February to April, and nearly the same results gained as with fall sowing, but with a little more trouble. Should these spring grown plants be too small for flowering before midsummer, they will be all the more rewarding in the fall months for not having flowered profusely in the spring.

PASSION FLOWER—PASSIFLORA *(Greenhouse Perennial, 35, 50, 90°).*

Climbing plants for the greenhouse and window that possess a pleasing appearance, both in the foliage, form of growth and in the flowers. They withstand the dry heat of dwellings better than the average of plants; are frequently planted permanently in the conservatory to climb along the rafters, for which purpose they are well suited and very ornamental.

PELARGONIUM—LADY WASHINGTON GERANIUM *(Greenhouse Perennial, 33, 45 to 55, 90°).*

A distinct division of the Geranium family (popularly speaking, for, in a botanical sense, the Geraniums are Pelargoniums), which are only suitable for pot culture, producing flowers of an extremely high rank of beauty and color. The plant is in appearance somewhat similar to the common Horseshoe or Scarlet Geranium, but the flowers, although of similar form, are much larger, averaging about two inches across, and are of the richest colors, and shades of colors, imaginable, ranging from purest white, through carmine, crimson, rosy pink, vermillion, to the darkest maroon, and through the intervening shades for the ground work, and upon these the most exquisite veinings and delicate shadings, all on petals of the finest satin-like texture, yet, of such a thickness that but the deepest markings run through them, the under side being generally a tinted white, or a lighter and uniform shade of the predominating color of the flower. The Pelargonium is not so valuable a window plant as some of the Geraniums, for, although of free, healthy growth, under any circumstances, it is here inclined to be a shy bloomer, but, as a spring and early summer flowering plant in the conservatory, all the varieties possess the greatest value, and bloom with exceeding freedom. No conservatory can be considered well stocked without some of these plants in the collection. After the plants have flowered in summer they should be given a rest of two months by almost entirely withholding water from them. At the end of this time they should be cut back and be repotted into fresh soil of a fertile nature, first soaking the ball of old earth in which they have been growing, and removing all that can be taken off, without mutilating the roots. Water may be freely applied from this time on. During winter the plants should be placed in a light situation, and given sufficient space to enable the air and light to reach all the foliage. Due attention should be paid to pinching back any strong growing shoots, and neat stakes should be provided. They propagate readily from cuttings. The end shoots obtained in pruning back plants after their annual rest, are most suitable for striking, and strong plants can be grown from these by spring, if they are repotted as required during winter.

Arcadian Prince, deep glowing rosy crimson, slightly penciled with maroon; an excellent grower and free bloomer. *Augusta Odier*, an exceedingly rich, carmine-veined variety. *Beadsman*, pink, maroon spots. *B:lle Blon:te*, white, edged and penciled with carmine, and spotted with maroon. *Bianca*, shell tinted pink, with dark spots running through crimson to pink, on two petals. *Captivation*, pure white, with striking spots of dark maroon. *Diadematum*, bright crimson pink, penciled with maroon. *Dr. Andre*, blush pink ground, the margins of the petals elegantly fringed. *Gen. Taylor*, a free flowering carmine pink variety, slightly marked with maroon on two petals; a superb variety. *Gloris de Belleview*, light, veined crimson, with blackish maroon spots; fine. *James Odier*, upper petals white, under shell-tinted with maroon markings. *Lavina*, pure white, with the lower petals distinctly marked with maroon and edged with crimson. *Marksman*, white ground, profusely marked and stained with purplish crimson. *Madella D'Or*, darkest crimson, with darker spots and light center; exceedingly rich. *Mazinella*, pink, crimson and maroon. *Norma*, light lilac on white, with dark spots. *Sir Casper*, light pink, blotched with maroon and crimson. *White Lady*, a pure white variety, the flowers of which, although freely produced, are rather below the average in size.

Fig. 52. Double Neapolitan Violets. See page 81.

PENSTEMON (*Greenhouse Perennial, 30, 45, 75°*).

A class of nearly hardy plants suitable for the flower garden and pot culture. They bloom for a long time. The flowers are produced in spikes of Foxglove-like form, very nicely shaded and mottled. Can be taken up in the fall and preserved in a cold-pit or the cool end of a conservatory or in the cellar during winter. Propagate readily from cuttings.

PETUNIA (*Half-Hardy Annual or Greenhouse Perennial, 33, 50, 85°*).

For out-door decoration in summer there are few plants that excel this class. They commence to flower early and continue a mass of bloom the whole summer and until after frosts. There are both double and single varieties, the former usually being increased from cuttings and treated as greenhouse perennials in winter, and the latter as annuals, raising them from seed each spring, although the best of these can also be perpetuated very profitably from cuttings, thus insuring the purity of any desirable strain. Double varieties can also be raised from seed, but only a small percentage of even the most carefully saved seed can be depended upon to come double. Aside from the great value of the entire family as bedding plants, the double varieties especially are very satisfactory if grown in rich soil in pots, and the stronger growing single varieties are excellent for planting in hanging baskets and vases for trailing over the edges. For this purpose the seed should be sown as early as March. For ordinary summer decoration the seed may be sown in a hot-bed, cold-frame or prepared seed-bed, transplanting the seedling plants eighteen inches apart in the garden, in May, or sowings may be made where the plants are desired, which will do quite as well, excepting that these will not flower within several weeks as early as the others.

The most desirable varieties among the double Petunias are : *Beauty*, rich crimson and white striped; sometimes sports. *Cleopatra*, white, blotched with violet crimson. *Delicata*, lavender and blush. *Maiden's Blush*, light rosy pink; very beautiful, and a free bloomer. *Queen of Whites*, pure white; very double; somewhat resembling a white Carnation, but larger. *Wm. White*, crimson and white. *Wm. Heines*, dark violet crimson. Among the single varieties which may be reared from seed, the following are prominent for their superiority : *Countess of Ellesmore*, rosy carmine, with white throat; an exceedingly desirable variety, coming true from seed. In the large flowering (Grandiflora) section : *Green Margined*, crimson color, white throat, green edge. *Inimitable*, purplish red, spotted and margined with white. *Kermesina*, large crimson. *Maculata*, purple and crimson, spotted white. *Venosa*, beautiful veined variety.

Fig. 53. Phlox Drummondii.

PHLOX *(Half-Hardy Annuals and Hardy Perennials).*

This family, in its several divisions, embraces many varieties of garden plants of the highest value to the amateur or commercial florist. Throughout they are of fine habit and vigorous growth, producing flowers of very attractive colors in great profusion, the plants thriving in any garden soil, and with the most ordinary attention. On account of these desirable qualities they are recommendable to cultivators of little experience, as there is scarcely any danger of failure to realize successful results with their cultivation.

PHLOX DRUMMONDII.—Among seed-grown annuals for the garden the Phlox Drummondii stands without a rival for brilliancy of colors and continual display. It is to this class, what the Verbena and Geranium are to tender greenhouse bedding plants, and it is even a most formidable rival of these distinct and brilliant flowering plants, when effect is taken into consideration; while with calculating on the small outlay necessary to procure an abundance of seed, the readiness with which it is cultivated from seed, and its general attractiveness, either in ordinary beds or in ribbons and masses, it is deserving of attention from cultivators generally as a showy bedding plant of the greatest importance, and also as one of the best for cut flowers, the flowers being produced on conveniently long stems. The different varieties afford many distinct and striking colors, such as pure white, white with purple eye, deep blood purple, brilliant scarlet, beautiful rose color, rose with white eye, dark violet with white eye, red with white eye, crimson striped with white, slate color, and many others, all of which come true to color from seed.

The seed may be sown either in the hot-bed, cold-frame or open ground. The plants should stand from nine to twelve inches apart. They commence flowering early and continue to produce an abundance of bloom until towards winter, especially if not allowed to seed.

HARDY UPRIGHT PHLOXES.—These are hardy herbaceous perennials, and among the most useful and showy in cultivation. The flowers are produced in great profusion, on upright stems from one to three feet high, in the summer and fall months. The plants are perfectly hardy, and will thrive in any garden soil. After they have attained some size, the roots may be taken up in the fall or spring, be divided and reset. The following is a desirable list of varieties:

Alexandriena Varennes, deep rose. *Delecata,* rich dark purplish crimson. *Glorie de Nieully,* brilliant salmon red. *Harlequin,* brilliant crimson, somewhat mottled. *Hector Rouillard,* distinctly striped crimson and rose. *L. Avenir,* salmon and red; very fine. *Mad. Amezi Pothier,* pink with deep red eye. *Mad. Bellvenue,* deep rose, crimson center. *Mad. Bernian,* rosy purple, crimson eye. *Mad. de Chambrey,* large rosy purple, distinct dark eye. *Mad. de Wendall,* almost pure white, crimson eye. *Mad. Masson,* crimson, petals edged and striped with purplish rose. *Mad. Pepin,* rose, with salmon center and crimson eye; distinct. *Mad. Van Houtte,* light pink with bright crimson eye. *Mons. Duffe,* brilliant crimson. *Napoleon,* pure white distinctly striped with purple. *Roi des Roses,* rosy purple with bright crimson eye. *Startler,* striped rose. *Venus,* blush with carmine eye. *Victor Hugo,* striking purplish crimson.

HARDY PROCUMBENT PHLOXES (Moss Pink).—These differ from the other sections of the family, in being of creeping habit, with small pointed leaves. They produce their pretty flowers in May, at which time the prostrate plants are literally covered with bloom. Of the easiest culture. Propagate by division.

P. Setacea, pink flowers in immense numbers. *P. Setacea alba,* pure white, similar in form and growth to the preceding variety, and very attractive.

PILEA—ARTILLERY PLANT *(Greenhouse Perennial, 35, 50, 80°).*

Unique plants, with graceful frond-like leaves, which, when in flower, produce a snapping sound if water is thrown upon them. They are useful either as pot plants or for planting in baskets, vases, Ferneries, etc., being in either case easy to manage. Propagate from cuttings.

PINK, GARDEN OR FLORIST'S—*(Hardy Perennial).*

A class of hardy plants for the garden that pertain to the Dianthus family. They much resemble Carnations, but are more dwarf. The flowers are perfectly double, clove scented, and embrace numerous colors in the different varieties, including pure white, carmine, pink, etc., in some of which striking deep rose, maroon, deep carmine and other colors appear in the center of the flower or distinctly on each petal. Some are also beautifully fringed. The plants may be propagated by cuttings or by layers, and will thrive in any garden soil.

PURE WHITE HARDY PINKS.—*Sarah Howard,* a fragrant, double, pure white, free flowering summer and fall Pink, not entirely hardy, but with slight protection, very desirable; exceedingly valuable for bouquet making. *Alba fimbriata,* a double white early spring flowering sort, of good form and substance, being fringed and very fragrant; grown extensively by florists for bouquet flowers; perfectly hardy and unequaled for forcing in pots in winter, for which purpose any of the ordinary plants from the garden may be taken up and potted in the fall without previous treatment. For forcing, 32, 50, 80°.

PLUMBAGO CAPENSIS *(Greenhouse Perennial, 35, 50, 85°).*

A shrubby greenhouse pot plant, also suitable for window culture, producing large trusses of azure blue flowers, during fall and winter months. It flowers freely in plants six inches high, and as the colors of its flowers is rare, it is a desirable addition to any collection.

POINSETTIA PULCHERRIMA *(Greenhouse Perennial, 35, 55 to 65, 100°).*

A tropical plant of remarkable growth, and possessed of gorgeous beauty when in bloom. The flower, or rather the bracts or leaves that surround the flower proper, in well grown specimens attain a diameter of one foot, and of the most dazzling scarlet. The plants require a warm place to develop the flower heads, which appear in December and January, but with this requirement supplied, they are of the easiest culture. Sandy soil suits them best. After their flowering season they should receive only enough water to prevent the soil from becoming powder dry, and the plants may be set under the staging until spring when they may be repotted, plunging the pots in soil in the open ground, until the time of returning them under glass, which should be in September.

POLYANTHUS—PRIMULA ELATIOR, CUPS AND SAUCERS *(Hardy Perennial).*

Pretty, early flowering, hardy garden plants that are found in many collections. They flower mostly in May. The flowers appear in trusses on erect stems, and embrace various colors, including brown with yellow eye and delicate yellow edge, rich brown, almost black, either shaded or plain, various combinations of crimson, yellow, sulphur, etc. May be increased by division, and also from seed. They delight in a light loamy soil and are benefited by a covering of leaves or other material through winter.

POMEGRANATE, DWARF *(Almost Hardy Shrubby Perennial).*

The fruit bearing Pomegranate is a native of Asia, and is much cultivated in warm countries. The dwarf, flowering kind is valuable for pot culture, bearing brilliant orange scarlet flowers of leathery substance. It is a deciduous plant, and with pot culture may be stored in a cellar, cold-pit, or under the staging in the conservatory during winter, and until April, when it should be brought to light and started into growth. In the Southern States the dwarf Pomegranate is hardy with slight protection.

POPPY—PAPAVER *(Hardy Annuals and Hardy Perennials).*

Showy and well known border flowers, apt to be despised through ignorance of the really good qualities of improved varieties. The annual varieties are readily grown from seed, which should be sown where the plants are wanted. Among the perennial sorts *P. Bracteatum* is a scarlet variety. *P. Croceum,* orange; an early and free bloomer. *P. Orientale* (Oriental Poppy), large, orange red; flowering the fore part of summer. These may also be reared from seed or by division.

PORTULACA *(Half-Hardy Annual).*

Exceedingly brilliant and popular low growing annuals of the easiest culture. There are both double and single varieties, including white, rose, golden, orange, crimson, scarlet, rosy purple and other colors, besides beautifully striped varieties. The Double Portulacas are of remarkable beauty, being as double and as perfect as a fine Rose. All luxuriate in an exposed sunny situation, and produce throughout the summer their distinct and showy flowers in the greatest profusion, on which account they possess very high value for planting in masses or in ribbon lines, as well as for other purposes in adorning the grounds and garden. A bed of either the double or single varieties, but especially of the former, will form as attractive an object with their brilliant colors as can be introduced, particularly in bright sunny weather. Are grown with readiness from seed, which may be sown early in the open ground, or in the hot-bed, or pots in the window, and afterwards setting the young seedlings about eight inches apart in the garden. The seeds saved from double flowers will not all produce perfectly double flowers, although a large enough percentage may be depended upon to be satisfactory.

POTENTILLA—CINQUE FOIL *(Hardy Perennial).*

An extensive genus, mostly natives of the temperate zones, some of which are worthy of cultivation, while many are ranked among weeds. The foliage of nearly all the varieties very closely resembles that of the strawberry plant. There are in cultivation varieties with dark crimson, orange scarlet, blood red, blush and salmon, red shaded with maroon, colored flowers, which, although not as showy as those of some other plants, they possess a pleasing beauty and are produced with little intermission through the entire season. Succeed in any garden soil, and are increased either from seed or by dividing the roots.

PRIMROSE—PRIMULA *(Greenhouse Perennial, 35, 50, 85°).*

This is a most valuable class of plants for pot culture, either in the conservatory or window. They grow less than one foot in height and produce an immense number of the purest white and other colored flowers during fall, winter and spring. There is a Double White variety, which is extensively grown for winter flowers by florists. The flowers are an inch across, perfectly double, and of the purest white. This variety is increased with some difficulty by division and from cuttings in the spring; is rather impatient of ill-treatment, and will not do as well in the window as the single varieties. It requires a fine, rich soil, containing considerable sand, and does not bear to be crowded closely among other plants. In the summer it should be grown under glass, heavily coated with a wash of quick-lime and water. During winter the glass should also be kept slightly whitened, and as uniform a temperature as possible be maintained. Water may be freely applied, but sprinkling the leaves and flower-stems should be avoided as much as possible. The Single varieties are reared from seed, which is sown in summer, usually. These include flowers of white, rose, and crimson colors, and also some with finely fimbriated edges. The directions given for managing the double Primrose are applicable to the single varieties.

PYRETHRUM. See Feverfew.

RANUNCULUS *(Hardy Perennials).*

RANUNCULUS ACRIS FLORE PLENO (Butter Cup, Crowfoot).—A hardy herbaceous perennial that is quite common. The flowers are double, of pretty, glossy yellow color, produced on upright stems, two feet high, in June and July. Will thrive in any soil, and when once introduced in a garden, there is no difficulty in keeping it, as it grows freely and propagates by division very easily.

RANUNCULUS ASIATICUS. is a section which affords some of the most splendid flowers in cultivation, but, unfortunately, our winters are too severe to rear them, without great difficulty, in the open ground, on which account their culture is generally precluded, except in the window and conservatory, where they may be grown by observing the directions given for cultivating the Hyacinth and other Hardy Bulbs, etc., on page 21.

RHODANTHE *(Half-Hardy Annual).*

A beautiful, though somewhat delicate, genus of Everlasting flowers, grown from seed, which should be started in the house.

R. atrosanguinea is a distinct variety, of dwarfish, branching habit, the flowers of which are deep purple and violet, with magenta ray scales. *R. maculata*, rosy purple, with yellow disc; of quite strong growth and large flowers. *R. maculata alba*, similar to the preceding, except that the flowers are pure white, with yellow disc. This is the finest, pure white, everlasting in cultivation. *R. Manglesii*, bright rosy color, and silvery calyx; rather delicate for the open ground, but succeeds finely as a pot plant.

Fig. 54. Verbenas. See page 81.

RICHARDIA ALBA MACULATA *(Tender Bulb).*

A plant belonging to the same order as the Calla, with beautifully spotted leaves. It flowers during the summer months, either in pots or if planted out in the open border. The flowers are shaped like those of the Calla, and are white, shaded with violet inside. It is a deciduous plant, to be kept dry in winter in the cellar or under the bench of the conservatory, and started in spring like a Dahlia.

RICINUS—Castor Oil Bean *(Half-Hardy Annual).*

A genus of ornamental seed-grown plants of stately growth, and with picturesque foliage, that are highly useful for planting, either singly or in groups, about the lawn or garden, or with other strong growing plants, possessing striking foliage or flowers, such as Cannas, Caladiums, Japanese Striped Maize, Hollyhocks, Helianthus, etc. The seeds may be planted in the open ground in May, or may be started a month earlier in pots, in the hot-bed or window, thus securing showy plants some weeks earlier. Young plants will not bear much moisture or cold.

ROSE. See pages 25 to 33.

ROSEMARY—ROSEMARIANUS OFFICINALIS *(Greenhouse Perennial, 33, 45 to 55, 85°).*
A common sweet scented plant, of erect habit, much cultivated as a house plant. It thrives with the most ordinary care, and is generally prized by all who cultivate it.

SALPIGLOSSIS *(Half-Hardy Annual).*
Beautiful annuals for the garden, with funnel-shaped flowers, richly colored, delicately veined and marbled. On close examination the blossoms will be found to have a rich, velvety softness seldom seen in other flowers. But for the fact that the plants are of somewhat slender and straggling growth, they would be exceedingly desirable. Seed may be sown in the open border. The plants should stand about eight inches apart.

SALVIA—SAGE *(Greenhouse Perennial, 33, 45 to 50, 80°).*
A family of late summer flowering plants, suitable for the garden. They are of robust growth, easily cultivated in any soil, and form very attractive plants when in bloom. Easily increased from cuttings, and some varieties from seed; the plants may be lifted in the fall and kept in a growing condition, either in a light cellar, the window or conservatory, until February, when new stock may be propagated for spring planting.
S. Grahami Purpurea, purplish crimson. *S. Officinalis Tricolor,* a beautiful variegated variety of the common Sage; foliage blotched with white, green and sometimes pink; dwarf, bushy habit; fine for bedding. *S. Patens,* flowers of the richest and most distinct blue; excellent for pot culture. *S. Splendens,* a superb fall flowering bedding plant, growing to a height of two to three feet, and completely covered with spikes of dazzling scarlet flowers, causing it while in bloom to be the most attractive plant in the garden. A sharp lookout should be kept for the Green-fly on this plant, in the winter, as it is perhaps more liable to attacks from this insect than any other plant in cultivation. *S. Splendens alba,* a pure white variety, similar in form of growth and flowers to the preceding. An excellent plant for decorating the conservatory and window in autumn, if grown in a good sized pot.

SANCHEZIA NOBILIS VARIEGATA *(Greenhouse Perennial, 35, 50 to 90°).*
A highly ornamental plant of good habit and vigorous growth, producing large leaves of intense green, the veins of which are broadly margined with golden yellow. As a handsome, variegated, foliage plant of easy culture in pots, it is very desirable, particularly in a warm conservatory. A light, rich soil suits it the best.

SCABIOSA—MOURNING BRIDE *(Half-Hardy Annual).*
A garden plant of considerable value, grown from seed. There are tall and dwarf kinds, the former attaining a height of two feet; the dwarf, one-half of this height, but both are of free growth and produce distinct flowers of many colors and shades, from white, through lilac, brick color, dark purple, etc., down to almost jet black; these are produced on long, straight stems, which, with being neat and pretty, render them exceedingly useful for cutting for summer bouquets. In flower from July to October. The seed may be sown early in the open ground, or started in heat, afterwards setting the seedlings a foot or fifteen inches apart in the garden.
S. nana fl. pl., a dwarf variety, somewhat distinct, the flowers of which are quite double and globular, extending through all the colors of the tribe. *S. Stellata* (Starry Scabiosa). The petals, or rather seed vessels, of this variety are of peculiar scaly texture, and when dried are useful for arranging with the everlastings and dried grasses into winter bouquets.

SEDUM—STONE CROP *(Hardy Perennials, principally).*
Mostly garden plants, with thick succulent leaves, and very tenacious of existence; the common Live-for-Ever belonging to the genus. Some of the varieties are of erect habit, many of which are exceedingly attractive in the garden, while others are creeping and trailing, being very useful for cultivating in pots in the window or conservatory, or for planting in baskets, vases, etc., to droop over the edge. Among the latter *S. Seboldii,* with grayish green foliage and wiry-like stems, and *S. Seboldii variegata,* similar to the preceding, except that the leaves are varigated with yellow, are considered the best. Will thrive in any soil and progagate readily by division or from cuttings, which, of some varieties, will root if simply laid where it is damp.

SENSITIVE PLANT. See Mimosa Sensitiva.

SMILAX. See Myrsyphyllum Asparagoides.

SNAP-DRAGON. See Antirrhinum.

SNOWDROP. See Galanthus.

SOLANUM—JERUSALEM CHERRY, ETC. *(Greenhouse Perennial, 33, 45 to 55, 90°).*
A family of plants including several useful varieties, for pot culture in the window and conservatory and also for bedding. They are of the easiest possible culture, thriving in any soil and under apparently adverse circumstances. All may be readily raised from cuttings, and the fruit bearing variety from seed.
S. Jasminoides, of neat climbing habit, with small, dark green foliage and pure white flowers; suitable for training to trellis or pillars in the conservatory. *S. Pseudo-Capsicum,* the well known

Jerusalem Cherry, producing an immense crop of scarlet, cherry-like fruit, from early in the fall until after Christmas. Plants grown from seed are more productive of fruit the first season, than those struck from cuttings, or those several years old. Sow in the spring for fall bloom, and bring forward during summer either in ample sized pots, plunged in the open air, or else by planting out and taking up and potting the plants in September. *S. Pseudo-Capsicum fol. var.* is a dwarf variety of the above. Aside of its other good qualities, the foliage is margined with sulphur yellow to half the depth of the leaves. Whether used as a house plant, for bedding, or for vase or basket decoration, it is a valuable plant.

SPIREA *(Hardy Herbaceous Perennials and Shrubs).*

A genus containing a large number of species, including herbaceous plants and shrubs, natives of Europe, Asia, and America. They are all hardy, and produce showy flowers, usually in heads, their prevailing colors being white, pink, crimson, etc. Of the easiest culture in any garden soil, the herbaceous varieties propagating by division of the roots. The Astilbe Japonica, which is separately treated on, on page 39, belongs to this family. *S. Filipendula Pleno* is a highly esteemed variety, with deep green foliage of beautiful form, and pure white clusters of bloom, produced in June on stems from one to two feet high There is also a variety with variegated foliage and whitish flowers.

STATICE MARITIMA—Thrift, Sea Pink *(Hardy Herbaceous Perennial).*

A low growing plant of dense growth, which is valued for edging beds, walks, etc., being one of the best in cultivation for this purpose. It grows rapidly in any garden soil, and can be multiplied to any desired extent almost, yet does not partake of a weedy character in any way. The plants grow less than six inches high; are very compact, with narrow deep green leaves, and little heads of pink flowers in June and July. Should be taken up once every few years, and be divided and reset.

STEVIA *(Greenhouse Perennial, 33, 45, 85°).*

The Stevias, although botanically distinct from Eupatoriums (see Eupatorium, page 52), are, in points of free growing and winter flowering qualities and their general requirements, almost precisely the same as that family of plants, being with them of the easiest culture and a superior class of plants for the conservatory, and also useful for window culture. For their management, follow directions given for that family.

Compacta, an early flowering variety, with large compact heads of pure white flowers; continues in flowers nearly all winter, and longer than any other variety of either Stevia or Eupatorium. *Serrata,* a free flowering variety, blooming most freely about the holidays. The flowers are white and arranged loosely and gracefully along the stem.

STOCK—Gillyflower *(Half-Hardy Annuals, Biennials and Perennials).*

A genus of half-shrubby plants grown from seed, which produce spikes of elegant fragrant single and double flowers of many desirable and showy colors, including pure white. The plants are in no respect delicate, are easily reared, and in the different sections afford varieties of the greatest value, either for bedding or for pot culture in the window, the conservatory (temperature, 33, 45 to 55, 80°) or the open-air plant stand. All kinds of Stocks should be transplanted from the seed pots or beds in which they are started while they are quite small, as their slender roots soon extend to such a distance that the plants cannot be taken up without loss of fine rootlets, and consequent injury.

Ten Week Stocks.—These are important annuals ranking in general desirability as garden plants with the Aster, Balsam, Phlox Drummondii, Portulaca, Zinnia, etc., but are superior to either of these in their admirable adaptability to pot culture for blooming either in summer or winter. The section includes varieties, ranging in growth from one-half to one and one-half feet in height, which embrace a large variety of colors, such as white, bright crimson, carmine, blue, lilac, chamois, rose, blood-red, yellow, violet, purple and various shades of these, most of which are exceedingly pure, striking and fragrant, and a large percentage of the plants will produce flowers perfectly double. They delight in any well enriched soil. For summer flowering the seeds may be sown in the hot-bed or cold-frame in April, or the open ground in May, allowing the plants to stand twelve inches apart. For winter flowering, sow in July, August or September, and cultivate in pots in the open ground until cool autumn weather, when they should be moved under protection, but still treated to an abundance of fresh air as late in the season as possible, and also frequently in winter. During their flowering season in pots, they will be benefited by occasional waterings with weak liquid manure.

Autumnal or Intermediate Stocks.—This section are prized on account of their flowering late in the autumn and winter, which necessitates that they be grown in pots, and brought into the window or conservatory for blooming. For this purpose the seeds should be sown in the spring. Seeds may also be sown in July or August, for plants to flower in the spring. A large number of bright and desirable colors are embraced.

Emperor or Imperial Stocks.—This desirable class of Stocks are better suited for pot culture then for bedding, and are perennial in habit, frequently lasting for several years. If the seeds are sown in spring they will bloom in autumn, while for spring flowering they should be sown in July and August. The colors are white, rose and crimson, and the plants attain a height of eighteen inches.

BROMPTON STOCKS.—The Brompton Stocks are biennial in habit, flowering in the winter or spring, from seed sown the previous spring, in the window or conservatory, not being hardy enough to endure our winters in the open ground. By wintering the plants in a place sufficiently cool not to excite them into free growth and flowering, they may be planted into the border. early in the spring and will flower handsomely during summer. If a good quality of seed is sown, more than one-half may be expected to produce double flowers. The flowers vary from straw color to pure white, and rose to deep purple and violet.

SUNFLOWER. See Helianthus.

SWEET PEA—LATHYRUS *(Hardy Annuals and Perennials).* See Fig. 55.

The flowering annual Peas are desirable and popular plants for the garden; excellent for bouquets and cut flowers, and are commended as one of the most essential to every collection. They are among the most fragrant of all the garden flowers, and a great variety of shades and colors are afforded, such as white, rose and white, purple and white, scarlet, scarlet striped with white, black, black with light blue, brownish purple, etc. Being a perfectly hardy annual, seed may be sown as early in spring as the soil can be prepared. Sow in clumps, groups, or drills, and place sticks or other fixtures for the Peas to run upon, and treat the same as the common garden Pea. By cutting the flowers as fast as they bloom the plants will continue prolific all season.

PERENNIAL PEA (Everlasting Pea).—A beautiful climbing perennial, easily grown from seed, or may be increased by dividing the roots of old plants. The flowers are red, white, rose-colored, etc., and are produced in clusters in long succession. An excellent plant for training to trellis, or an arbor, and is hardy.

SWEET WILLIAM. See Dianthus.

TAGETES SIGNATA PUMILIA. See Marigold.

THUNBERGIA *(Tender Annual).*

Trailing and climbing plants for conservatory and window culture, which are among our most valuable basket plants in protected situations, and are also well suited for bedding. The flowers are large, round, single and embrace peculiarly attractive colors, which are certain to be admired, being yellow, orange and buff in the different varieties, with an intensely dark eye of large size; there is also a pure white variety. The seeds should be started early, in a warm place; of slow growth while young, but as warm weather comes on the plants advance rapidly and flower constantly.

TIGRIDIA—TIGER FLOWER *(Tender Bulbous Perennial).*

A bulbous plant for the garden, producing beautiful and curious large flowers for a long time in summer. Their colors in different varieties embrace orange and scarlet with golden yellow variegations, and are distinctly spotted with black. The bulbs may be planted in May in warm situations, and should be lifted again early in October. After allowing them to dry, pack in dry sand or sawdust and store away from frosts—and mice, 1 might add, who will devour them if an opportunity is afforded—until time of planting in spring.

TROPÆOLUM—NASTURTIUM *(Half-Hardy Annuals and Greenhouse Perennials, 35, 50, 90°).*

A well-known genus, affording plants of strong growing and free flowering habits, some of which are dwarf and others climbers. The flowers are attractive and showy in all the varieties, the prevailing colors being dark crimson, brilliant scarlet, dark orange, sulphur spotted with maroon, etc. There is a double flowering variety, of orange scarlet color, which, with Star of Fire and varieties belonging to the Lobbianum section, are mostly cultivated as perennials, being increased by cuttings.

T. Star of Fire is an exceedingly useful and easily cultivated variety for pot culture in the conservatory, producing dazzling flowers in the greatest profusion, and climbing freely on trellis, pillar or rafters, if planted in a large pot. By starting with young plants of this variety in the spring, keeping them in pots, and placing in a light situation in the conservatory, each plant will produce hundreds of flowers from November until spring, of the following winter. The varieties which come under the head Nasturtium, are grown from seed planted either in open ground or in heat, and afterwards set in the garden. Those, classed with *T. Majus*, being climbers of rapid growth, make an excellent covering for old walls, trellises, etc.; while the varieties of *T. Minus* (Dwarf Nasturtiums), from their close, compact growth and rich colored flowers, are suitable for bedding purposes.

TROPÆOLUM PEREGRINUM (Canary Bird flower).—This is a beautiful climber, with fine cut foliage, the flowers of which are a bright Canary-yellow, and when half open have a pretty and fanciful likeness to little birds. The plants are well adapted for covering trellises, etc., and are easily grown from the seed, which may be sown directly where they are required, or in heat, afterwards transplanting the seedlings. In flower from July until frosts.

TULIP *(Hardy Bulb).*

The Tulip family, in some of its varieties at least, is too well known to require any description, being esteemed for its hardiness, ease of culture in any soil, the amazing brilliancy of its flowers which are produced in spring, and other good qualities.   The family consists of numerous classes, including the Early and Late Flowering, both double and single, Parrot, Duc Van Thol, Bizarres and Byblooms, in different varieties and colors, all of which are highly desirable. The gorgeous coloring in many of the improved varieties is remarkable, and a superiority can be claimed for the family in this respect over any other in cultivation to an extent. Among the large and most double varieties, as well as the single, are to be found distinct, pure white, pure white striped with rose, intense scarlet, velvety crimson, rich bright yellow, glittering red, and many other colors.   Tulips should be planted in the autumn, as directed on pages 14–15, at a distance of five or six inches apart, giving the tall, late varieties even a little more distance, and all about five inches deep.   They are also very valuable for forcing in the window or conservatory in winter, like Hyacinths, Crocus, etc., and special directions for their management here, are given on page 21.

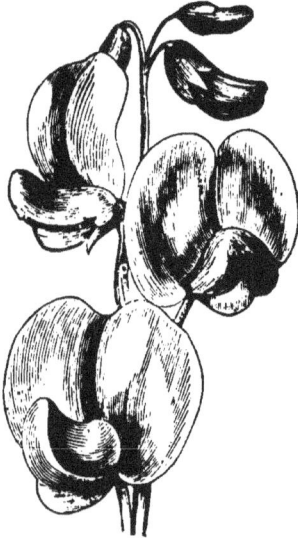

Fig. 55.   Flowering Pea.

Fig. 56.   Double Tuberose Flower.

TUBEROSE *(Tender Bulb).*

A bulbous plant, far less commonly grown than its abundant merits deserve, producing many beautiful pure white, wax-like, sweet-scented, double flowers, on long, upright stalks.   The only difficulty in the way of this magnificent flower being generally cultivated, is, that unless the tubers are started early, in artificial heat, our seasons in the North are not sufficiently long for it to flower in the open ground, and, then, unlike the Gladiolus, Tigridia, etc., the bulbs do not produce new bulbs each year for flowering the next.   They produce small bulblets freely, with each season's growth, but these must be cultivated—one, two or more years—before they will be sufficiently large for flowering.   The first difficulty may be overcome by starting the bulbs in pots, in a warm place, late in April and turning them into the garden soil the latter part of May.   Should frost, in September, threaten to destroy the flowers before all are expanded—as they open for several months in succession—no plants of the garden are easier to take up, and the roots may be carefully lifted and transplanted to pots, for removal to the conservatory or a warm, light window, where they can finish blooming.   Although the Tuberose requires considerable heat to flower well, growing bulbs may be transplanted, either in the spring or fall, with safety.   To secure bulbs for flowering, the young bulblets should, in the fall or spring, be removed from the old bulbs and be planted in a warm part of the garden, not earlier than the first of June, and given clean culture until the first of October.   This must be repeated each year with all that are desired for flowers, until they are strong enough to produce flowering shoots.   The bulbs of this plant require to be kept in a dry condition, where it is warm during winter.   The temperature should not fall far below 45°, else they may receive injury, by the germ of the next season's flowering shoot decaying, although the external appearance of the bulbs would not indicate it.   The Tuberose is susceptible of being managed to flower in winter by keeping the bulbs dry and starting them at any time, or at intervals for succession up to August 1st; but they require a situation where the thermometer, in the night, will indicate at least 60°, and ten or fifteen higher during the day, otherwise any attempt to force them will be fruitless.

TRITOMA UVARIA—Red-hot Poker *(nearly Hardy Perennial).*

This beautiful garden plant throws up, in September, numerous strong flower stems four feet in height, which are surmounted, each, with a spike of red and yellow flowers of exceedingly striking appearance. Although the Tritoma is nearly hardy in this latitude, it is better to take up the plants in autumn and keep in a cool cellar or cold-pit, covering the roots with earth or sand. Of the easiest culture, and will thrive in any garden soil.

VALLOTA PURPUREA *(Tender Bulb).*

This is a superb summer flowering bulb for pot culture, and also suitable for bedding. It is easily grown, and in August throws up its flowering shoots a foot or more high, each of which is surmounted by five to eight Lily-like flowers of brilliant scarlet color. During its season of growth the plant should be abundantly watered, and exposed to the sun as much as possible. In October water should be gradually withheld allowing them to become fully dry by November, in which condition they should be kept in any dry place, away from frost until March, when they may be started into growth, by applying water, for another season of flowering.

VERBENA *(Annual or Greenhouse Perennial, 33, 45, 80°).* See Fig. 54.

The Verbena is in every respect a desirable bedding plant, but of little use for pot culture. In the open air it is a rapid grower, an abundant bloomer, and the flowers in the varieties embrace colors and shades, varied without end almost, and exceedingly bright and attractive; indeed there is not a dull color to be found among them. Verbena plants set out in May require but a warm shower to start them into rapid growth, which in the hot weather of June will assume a spreading form, and the plant be continually in bloom. By August the upright single stem plant that was set in May, will have extended to three feet across, and will at all times be covered with scores of beautiful, bright, in some varieties, fragrant flowers. Verbenas will thrive in any soil, but, without exception, it should be in the highest state of fertility. I would particularly caution inexperienced growers against planting too close in the beds; three feet is near enough. Do not grow them on the same spot too often, as they are finer on fresh soil. After the plant has made some growth, the stems should be pegged down to the ground with hair-pins, or little sticks like matches, four inches long crossed over them. The Verbena is most generally increased from cuttings, although it can be easily reared from seed. The advantage of adopting the former method is, that the splendid named varieties can be maintained from year to year, while it can never be known what colors will come from the seed, besides the latter will also lack the fine form of the selected named varieties, each one of which, is likely to equal the best that could be reared among thousands, from seed. In winter, stock plants require a cool, light, airy situation, on which account it is a difficult matter to keep up healthy ones, except in the conservatory. Where it is desired to keep over stock it is better to start young plants for the purpose from cuttings, in September, than to take up and pot old plants. Propagation from these for bedding in the spring may be done at any time from January until the last of March, but the young plants should be given as much light and air as possible. To grow seedlings, sow in February, March or April, provide plenty of light and air, and never allow them to be crowded. Verbenas, if well hardened, will bear slight freezing without injury.

VERBENA MONTANA *(Hardy Verbena).*—This is a very pretty and perfectly hardy plant, for the garden. The flowers are similar in form to the tender varieties; of a bright rose color, changing to lilac, and are produced in great profusion all summer. Plant is of low spreading habit, and handsome.

VERONICA *(Half-Hardy Perennial, 30, 45, 75°).*

A class of plants blooming during the fall months, that are well adapted for bedding and pot culture. The flowers are borne on spikes from three to five inches in length, running through the various shades of purple, rose, lilac and white, and are attractive. The plants succeed in any soil, and when growing in the garden may be taken up and preserved in a cold-pit during winter, or may be kept in a cool part of the conservatory. There is a handsome variegated variety which is highly attractive, either as a pot, basket or vase plant, or for bedding.

VIRGINIAN STOCK—Malcolmia Maritima *(Hardy Annual).*

This beautiful little annual, notwithstanding its popular name, is a native of the shores of the Mediterranean. The seeds may be sown directly where the plants are wanted, early or at any time in the spring. The plants grow six inches high, and embrace in the respective varieties red, white and rose colored flowers. The flowers are small and distinct; are produced in great profusion on erect stems well above the plant, from early in the season until after frosts. Useful for massing and in ribbon beds, and may also be grown as an edging plant. The plants should stand three or four inches apart.

VIOLET *(Hardy Perennial).*

Well known hardy spring flowering plants, very highly esteemed for their earliness, and the rich refreshing fragrance of the flowers, which include several shades of violet-blue color, in the different varieties. There are double and single varieties, the former being most highly prized, although they lack somewhat in hardiness. These are forced to a very large extent, for winter flower, in all large cities where a good demand for cut flowers exists. Plants designed for this purpose, are grown in the open ground during summer, at a foot apart each way. In

6

September these are gone over, and the runners which start into growth about this time are removed. This operation is repeated every few weeks, and in October the plants are taken up and potted, or if to be forced in the conservatory they may be planted directly on the beds. The plants will not bear much confinement, and a crop of flowers can only be expected where plants are kept cool (32, 45, 75°) and treated to an abundance of fresh air. The double varieties may be wintered with entire safety in a cold-pit, or by receiving protection in the open ground. All delight in cool places, and a little shade. Propagate by division and cuttings.

WALL FLOWER—CHERIANTHUS CHEIRI *(Half-Hardy Perennial.)*

This is a well known plant, of the easiest culture from seed, and suitable for pot or garden culture. It commences flowering in the spring of the second season after sowing ; during the preceding winter should be kept in the cellar, cold-pit, or cool part of the conservatory. There are handsome double and single flowers, very fragrant, with orange and yellow colors predominating, and these shaded red, brown or violet.

WAX PLANT. See Hoya.

XERANTHEMUM *(Hardy Annual).*

A class of everlasting flowers, possessing considerable merit for drying for winter decoration. There are white and several shades of light purple flowers, which are double and borne on long substantial stems that retain their strength with drying. The plants are robust and easily grown from seed, which starts readily and may be sown in heat or where the plants are wanted.

Double Zinnia Flower.

ZINNIA, DOUBLE *(Half-Hardy Annual).*

The improved Double Zinnia of the present day is emphatically one of the most valuable annuals that can be grown, and one that is deserving of a place in every flower garden. The plant is robust, free-growing and exceedingly prolific, and may be reared from seed sown under glass, transplanting the plants when small, or in the open ground, as soon as danger from frost is over. The flowers are of beautiful form and texture, perfectly double in the best sorts, and afford white, scarlet, yellow, purple, salmon, violet and other colors in the different varieties. They begin to appear when the plants are very young, retain their attractiveness for a long time, and increase in number and beauty until hard frosts. Unfortunately the Zinnia, like many other choice double kinds of seed-grown plants, will only produce a certain percentage of double flowers from the best of seed. I generally set the plants six or seven inches apart, in rows twenty inches apart, and then as they come in flower thin out one half or more of the poorest, and thus retain only those of superior quality. This thinning must be done with caution, and several flowers should be allowed to form on a plant before deciding whether to pull it up or not, as plants which will in season produce the most double flowers, frequently show their first ones only partially double. The Zinnia will thrive in any garden soil.

THE FLORICULTURAL OPERATIONS OF THE YEAR, ARRANGED BY WEEKS.

The successful cultivation of plants and flowers depends largely on the performance of all operations connected therewith, at certain suitable times, and some kind of a reminder of the various ones, as they should occur, is serviceable to cultivators, especially to amateurs and others who devote only a small portion of time to floriculture. The following is an arrangement of the operations and work of the florist, during the year, into fifty-two parts, which are respectively adapted to the fifty-two weeks of a year. It is most perfect in its application, to latitudes between 42° and 43° (Buffalo, N. Y.), and persons living north and south should calculate upon the difference in the length, earliness and lateness of the season, between their own latitude and the above, in making use of the arrangement.

In dividing a year into fifty-two weekly parts, each part or week of the year, it is plain, will begin on the same day that the first week; or January 1, commences on; thus, if January 1 falls on Wednesday, so will January 8, January 15, and all the dates given below, the same being also true when the year begins with any other day of the week. The only exception to this is after Feb. 29, during a leap-year, and here the difference (one day) is so slight as to be of little consequence.

The matter under each weekly head is designed for the week commencing at the date given. Although nearly all the operations named may with safety be performed either at a time preceding or following the week under which they appear, those printed in *italics* are of general interest *at the season* in which they are given, without particular reference to the week they may be under. The following abbreviations are made use of : W. for Window, Con. for Conservatory, O. A. for Open Air, C. P. for Cold-Pit, W. F. for Winter Flowering. The small figures which appear frequently (thus [94]) refer to the pages where the subject is specially treated on.

January 1—First Week.

Read articles in preceding pages relative to the required temperature, adaptability and culture of each plant included in the collection....*Pay strict attention to airing*[20] *when the weather is mild, watering plants,*[14,20] *destroying insects, etc., in the Con.*[94] W.[90] *and C. P.*[94]—see Dec. 17 and Oct. 15....Give Callas,[43] hardy bulbs, in pots, etc.,[21] (see list Oct. 8) plenty of water....Fuchsias[53] at rest may be started....Repair at once any broken glass.

January 8—Second Week.

Give plants in W. extra protection,[20] *during severe nights*....Study and decide early what improvements would be desirable about the grounds; also to what extent you will engage in, or increase upon floriculture, during the coming year.:..Ascertain the number of plants, etc., required, and govern subsequent propagations, the procuring of plants, seeds, etc., accordingly.

January 15—Third Week.

Continue to bring in kinds named under Oct. 8, and Roses, etc., under Oct. 29....Tie up Hyacinths and other flowering plants.... *Keep Pelargoniums*[71] *near the light*....Syringe and wash plants,[87] etc.—see Nov. 26....See that dormant Canna and other tubers, etc., named under Oct. 8, are not suffering from any cause.

January 22—Fourth Week.

Seeds under Feb. 19 may be sown, for early. ....As bulbs pass out of flower, cut away the stalks....Keep the earth in pots mellow, etc. —see Dec. 17.

January 29—Fifth Week.

Make hot-bed sash, etc.—see Dec. 10.... *Study to improve plants, by pruning,*[81]....En-courage W. F. Roses, etc., by occasionally applying liquid manure.[88]

February 5—Sixth Week.

February is the month for propagating from cuttings,[15] all kinds of common soft-wooded plants in the W. and Con., for adornment, during the coming year, and nearly everything will strike readily, therefore, *as fast as suitable growth is afforded, make cuttings and propagate.* ....After Poinsettias[74] have flowered, give rest ....Provide seedling Plants named under Aug. 20, Oct. 29, with abundance of pot room, air, and light, and they will grow rapidly.

February 12—Seventh Week.

Continue to bring in, for forcing, kinds named under Oct. 8, and Roses, etc., under Oct. 29....Start Chrysanthemums[46] to propagate from....Provide an abundance of manure for future use.

February 19—Eighth Week.

Seeds of Pansy,[71] Verbena,[81] Salvia Splendens,[77] Petunia,[72] Stock,[78] Sweet Alyssum,[38] Mimulus,[18] Maurandia,[18] Ice Plant,[68] Sensitive Plant,[68] Delphinium,[50] Dianthus,[50] Antirrhinum,[38] may be sown to secure strong plants for spring and summer flowering ...*As the season advances plants will need more water, and should have an increase of air; be ever on guard against insects*—see Oct. 15, Dec. 17....Have clean pots and good soil on hand for newly started plants.

February 26—Ninth Week.

See that implements, vases, etc., for summer use are in repair....*Give all cuttings*[15] *close attention*....Perfect plans as alluded to under Jan. 8....Water abundantly plants being forced....*Give the Fernery*[31] *daily attention*—*see Dec. 24....See that climbers of all kinds have suitable support.*

March 5—Tenth Week.

See that a proper quantity of stock is coming on, either by propagation or otherwise. ....*Propagation from cuttings*[15] *should still go on for spring plants*, and Chrysanthemums,[46] Eupatoriums,[52] Stevias,[78] Roses,[25] Carnations,[44] Violets,[81] Libonia,[55] Laurustinus,[65] Jasminums,[64] W. F. Fuchsias,[55] Cytisus,[49] Chorozema,[46] Abutilons,[34] for W. F. be struck. ....*Pinch back*[87] *the shoots of newly started plants, to induce a stocky growth.* ....*Pot cuttings*[16] *soon as possible, after they are rooted.* ....Dormant Lemon Verbenas,[36] Richardias,[76] Gesneras,[59] Mimulus,[18] may be started to grow. ....*Out door work, such as grading,*[7] *trenching,*[12] *etc., should be commenced as early as the soil can be worked, but beware of digging stiff, loamy soil when it is wet.*

March 12—Eleventh Week.

Kinds named under Oct. 8, and Roses, etc., under Oct 29, may still be brought in. ....*Provide pot plants with as much room as possible.* ....See "*As the season advances,*" etc., Feb. 19, also Oct. 15 and Dec. 17.

March 19—Twelfth Week.

From the time Camellias[43] *start into growth until autumn they require to be shaded from the sun; will also need more water now,* and may be pruned if desirable. ....*Attend to airing Ferneries,*[21] see Dec. 24. ....Hot-beds[13] may be made for general purposes. ....If Anemone Hortensis[39] tubers have been kept over, plant at first opportunity.

March 26—Thirteenth Week.

Seeds of Gomphrena,[59] Cobœa,[47] Amaranthus,[36] Celosia,[44] Ipomœa,[62] Thunbergia,[79] Canary Bird Flower,[79] Canna,[44] may be sown in heat. ....*Hot-beds*[13] *should be very carefully aired, watered and protected; allow for the admittance of a little air during night time.* ....Lilies[65] may be started in pots. ....Oleanders,[70] Oranges and Lemons,[70] Cactus,[41] Pomegranates,[75] Hydrangeas,[62] may be started into new growth; repotting if needed. ....Calceolarias,[42] Cinerarias,[47] Pelargoniums,[71] may be treated to liquid manure[88] occasionally. ....*Give cuttings close attention; pot off early.* ....*Bedding and other plants in pots will do well in a good hot-bed.* ....Push outdoor work as the season will allow. Protection applied to beds, plants, etc., in the fall should be removed if not yet done. Sodding[9] may be done as soon as the ground is settled.

April 2—Fourteenth Week.

Cuttings may still be made of Verbenas,[81] Petunias,[72] Achryanthes,[35] Coleus,[47] Salvias,[77] Heliotropes,[60] Fuchsias,[53] German Ivy,[18] etc., for summer decoration, and the kinds named under March 5th for W. F. ....Seeds of Acroclinum,[35] Aster,[38] Balsam,[39] Browalia,[41] Cacalia,[41] Celosia,[44] Helichrysum,[60] Helipterum,[61] Japanese Maize,[64] Marigold,[67] Petunia,[72] Ricinus,[76] Phlox Drummondii,[73] Portulaca,[75] Scabiosa,[77] Stocks of all kinds,[78] Trapœolum,[79] Wall Flower,[82] Xeranthemum,[82] Double Zinnia,[62] and those named under Feb. 19 may be sown in heat[13]. ....If the soil is dry Hardy Perennials may be taken up, divided and reset, as required, and Lilies[65] be planted.

April 9—Fifteenth Week.

Not much fire heat is likely to be needed after this date in the Con.—*see "As the Season Advances,"* etc., *under Feb. 19.* ....Dahlias,[49] Caladiums,[42] Cannas,[44] Amaryllis,[37] Vallota,[81] may be started in heat. ....*As the soil becomes fit,* Candytuft,[44] Sweet Pea,[79] Convolvulus minor,[48] Mignonette,[68] Clarkia,[47] Sweet Alyssum,[36] Briza,[60] Coix Lachryma,[60] Lupinus,[67] may be sown[12] in the O. A. ....Overhaul plants remaining in the C. P. and give almost full exposure to air.

April 16—Sixteenth Week.

Keep watch of the seed-beds,[13] *watering when necessary, removing weeds, and thinning and transplanting plants that stand too close.* ....Watch for and destroy all insects [21]-[24] in the W. Con., etc., as with warm weather they multiply rapidly—see Dec. 17. ....If W. plants can be set outdoors during a warm shower they will be benefited. ....Early hanging baskets [5] may be planted. ....Sow lawns,[8] if ready. ....Divide and reset edgings of Statice[18]. ....Plant out Tritomas,[81] etc. ....*Secure plenty of loamy turf, manure, refuse hops, etc., for potting soil.*

April 23—Seventeenth Week.

Start Tuberose bulbs[80] in a warm place. ....Propagate Double White Primroses[75] by division. ...Cold-frames[13] may be sown with seeds named under April 2, etc. ...Hot-beds[13] may still be sown. ....If they have been well aired, Carnations,[44] Pinks,[74] Violets,[81] for W. F., etc., also Veronicas,[81] Penstemons,[72] Pansies,[71] may be planted out. ....Make a first planting of Gladiolus,[59] continue doing so at intervals of ten days or two weeks, until June 15.

April 30—Eighteenth Week.

Give an abundance of air to all plants; attend to pinching back[87]; will need close attention as regards watering, lest they suffer from drying out—see Feb. 19 and Dec. 17. ....See "Keep watch of Seed-beds," etc., April 16. ....*Mow the lawn*[8] *as soon as a little growth of grass has been made; repeat every two weeks or oftener, during the season.*

May 7—Nineteenth Week.

If well-hardened, Roses,[25] Verbenas,[81] and the hardiest annuals and other plants may be set out. ....See "Transplanting."[13]. ....Seeds may be sown[12] in the O. A.. of Animated Oats,[38] Amaranthus,[36] Amobium,[37] Antirrhinum,[38] Aster,[38] Browalia,[41] Cacalia,[41] Calendula,[43] Calliopsis,[43] Campanula,[44] Agrostemma,[36] Clarkia,[47] Morning Glory,[48] Erysimum,[48] Escholtzia,[52] Godetia,[59] Grasses,[60] Gypsophila,[60] Helianthus,[60] Helichrysum,[60] Leptosiphon,[65] Nemophila,[70] Pansy,[71] Petunia,[72] Phlox Drummondii,[73] Poppy,[75] Portulaca,[75] Salpiglossis,[77] Scabiosa,[77] Ten-week Stock,[78] Tropœolum,[79] Virginian Stock,[81] Xeranthemum,[82] Double Zinnia[62] besides those named under Aug. 13. ....The ventilators of the Con. may be kept open almost constantly. ....*See that no Red-Spider affect Roses, Fuchsias, etc.* This is a very small insect [21] [24] [31] appearing on the under-side of leaves, in large numbers, and causing them to turn brown and finally drop—see May 21. ...

Cut away flower stems of bulbs out of bloom, but let the leaves grow.

May 14—Twentieth Week.

The planting out of all but the most tender plants may go on... Plant out Dahlia tubers[49].... Sow seeds of Solanum[77] in pots, for autumn and winter decoration, and in the open air tender annuals, such as Balsam,[39]Calandrina,[42] Celosia,[44] Helipterum,[61] Japanese Maize,[64] Marigold,[67] Mirabilis.[68].... *Keep a lookout for Rose Saw-flies—see "Insects Injurious to Roses."*[31]

May 21—Twenty-first Week.

The glass of the Con. may be shaded,[34] except over Noisette and other Roses.[25] *These should be syringed frequently, as also should Camellias,[43] Fuchsias,[53] and other plants kept in during summer, to create moisture for preventing attacks of Red Spider. Water should also at all times be freely used on the walks and about the Con. The ventilators should be kept open....*Azaleas[39] may be repotted and moved out; also Agaves,[35] Caladiums,[42] Dracenas,[52] and other ornamental pot plants, designed for the lawn, etc..... Winter-flowering Roses,[25] Bouvardia,[41] Jasminums,[64] Poinsettias,[74] and those named March 5, to be grown in pots during summer, should be moved to the O. A., and carefully plunged in soil or other substance to prevent their drying out; each one should be placed on a stone, pot-shred or slate, to prevent angle worms entering through the hole below.... House plants[19] may be moved to summer quarters.... Vases,[17] hanging baskets,[11] etc., may be put out, and new ones still planted.... Fuchsias,[53] Geraniums,[55] Ageratums,[35] Cupheas,[48] Petunias,[79] Heliotropes,[60] etc., make handsome pot plants for fall blooming if propagated[15] now, and kept pinched back[87] for eight weeks.... Plant out Bouvardia,[41] started Dahlias,[49] Coleus,[47] also Tigridia,[79] Amaryllis,[37] Vallota,[81] and sow Ricinus,[76] Acroclinium,[35] Rhodanthe,[15] Ipomœa[62] seeds.... If not yet done, W. F. Fuchsias,[55] should be given rest.

May 28—Twenty-second Week.

Trapæolums,[79] and Heliotropes,[60] for W. F., may be propagated; also a general collection of such things as will be useful for winter decoration,[20] including plants with ornamental foliage, and for Ferneries,[91] also Ivies,[62] and the freest growing plants named under March 5 .... New lawns still to be sown,[8] should be seeded with as little delay as possible.... Any of the seeds named under May 7–14, etc., may still be sown in the O. A.... *Be prepared to destroy Rose Slugs,[31] if any appear*—see June 18, also July 9.

June 4—Twenty-third Week.

Planting of Geraniums,[55] Verbenas,[81] and all started bedding plants is still in order.... Set out young Tuberose bulblets[80].... Callas[43] should be given a rest of several months when done flowering.... *Keep Double White Primroses[15] in shade, and give plenty of space.*

June 11—Twenty-fourth Week.

Pinch back [14][87] Carnations,[44] Bouvardia,[41] and

other W. F. plants that require it[14].... After all plants for outdoors have been moved from the Con. it should be thoroughly cleared up for the summer.... Wash empty pots.... *Watch for and destroy Chafers[31] on Rose bushes.*

June 18—Twenty-fifth Week.

Peg down Verbenas,[81] and other trailing bedding plants.... *See "Summer Culture,"[14] "Watering Plants," etc.,[14] "Removal of Matured Flowers."[81].... Mow the lawn frequently. Maintain neatness in all parts of the grounds. ... Water hanging baskets,[11] vases,[11] pot plants,[14] etc., abundantly.... Syringe and use water freely in the Con., not neglecting Camellias.[43] Provide Sweet Pea,[79] Morning Glory,[48] and other climbers, with support, as needed.*

June 25—Twenty-sixth Week.

Re-pot, if necessary, Roses and other W. F. plants named and alluded to under May 21, and keep well watered and plunged.... Propagation[15] of plants named and alluded to under May 28, may still go on.... *As strong young shoots are formed layering[16] may be done.*

July 2—Twenty-seventh Week.

Any building or improvement of Conservatories which is contemplated, also repairing of glass, etc., should be done, to have them ready for plants in Sept. and Oct..... *Sweet Alyssum,[36] Ten-Week Stock,[78] and Mignonette,[68] may be sown for W. F....* Candytuft,[44] Mignonette,[68] Phlox,[73] Erisymum,[52] may be sown in O. A. for succession.

July 9—Twenty-eighth Week.

Keep edgings clipped, and cut the edges of grass borders occasionally.... Allow no weeds to grow either in the walks or beds.

July 16—Twenty-ninth Week.

Layering[16] of Carnations,[44] Pinks,[74] Roses,[25] etc., should receive attention where suitable growth is afforded—see June 11 and 18.

July 23—Thirtieth Week.

Should the season prove dry, Dahlias,[49] Carnations,[44] newly planted trees, etc., will be benefited by mulching.... Plants alluded to under May 28 may still be propagated[15].... Seeds of kinds named under Aug. 13 and 20 may be sown[12] thus early.

July 30—Thirty-first Week.

Pinch and use the knife freely on monthly Roses and all rapid growing plants, see "Pruning,"[31][88].... For potting soil, see April 16.... After done flowering give Pelargoniums[71] rest .... *For Rust on Roses,—see page 33.*

August 6—Thirty-second Week.

Callas[43] may be started to grow.... Keep flowering Dahlias, Gladiolus, Lilies, etc., tied to stakes.... The re-potting of Oleanders, etc., named under March 26, is seasonable, after they have made a growth.... Carnations,[44] designed for early flowers should receive their last heading back.

August 13—Thirty-third Week.

Winter-flowering Fuchsias[55] may be started. .... Propagation[15] of Geraniums and other plants alluded to under Sept. 10, may be begun. As they require it re-pot W. F. plants named and alluded to under May 21....Sow Seeds of Pansy,[71] Hollyhock,[61] Delphinum,[50] Dianthus,[50] Aquilegia,[38] Canterbury Bells,[44] Digitalis,[52] Lychnis,[67] Myosotis,[68] Perennial Poppy,[76] Lobelia Cardinalis,[67] Antirrhinum,[38] —*see June 18, also July 11.*

August 20—Thirty-fourth Week.

Sow,[13] for winter and spring decoration, Calceolaria,[49] Cineraria,[47] Cobœa Scandens,[47] Cyclamen,[49] Primula,[75] Smilax,[69] Ten-Week Stock[78]....*For drying everlastings, gather before fully expanded, tie in small bunches, and hang in the shade....In gathering seed, save that only from the best flowers.*

August 27—Thirty-fifth Week.

Provide pots, potting soil, fuel, etc....Lilium Candidum[65] may now be reset....*Layering[16] may still be kept up.*

September 3—Thirty-sixth Week.

Give Fuchsias[53] rest as they cease to flower. ....Remove runners, and cut back W. F. Violets[81]—see July 2.

September 10—Thirty-seventh Week.

Carnations[44] for W. F., also Tuberoses[80] not yet done flowering, may be taken up and potted....*Propagation[15] of a general stock of tender plants should be engaged in,* which are to be increased during the fall and winter for spring and later use. Those named under Oct. 1 may be deferred until then....Repot such W. F. plants named and alluded to under May 21 as require it.

September 17—Thirty-eighth Week.

Hardy Bulbs named under October 8 may be planted in the O. A.[14] or started for forcing[21] ....*Be on your guard against frosts, and protect for a week or two longer or take in, all W. F. plants, for the window or conservatory.* Vases, hanging baskets, and the showy pot plants named under May 21, may be left out longer by carefully protecting in cool and frosty nights.

September 24—Thirty-ninth Week.

See "Treatment of Plants designed for W. F.,"[14] also Roses[32].. . Pelargoniums[71] may be cut back and started into growth. *Give cuttings[16] close attention daily, and see "Keep watch of seed-beds," etc., April 16....*A little fire heat may be needed on cool, frosty nights —see Oct. 15.

October 1—Fortieth Week.

Ferneries[91] for winter adornment may be planted....Petunias,[72] Centaureas,[45] Carnations,[44] Pinks,[74] can be propagated better now than earlier ; Verbenas[81] strike well yet.... *Chrysanthemums[16] may be stimulated with liquid manure[81]....Pot cuttings,[16] soon as they are rooted; thin out, transplant or pot any seedlings which may require it....*Sow, for early plants next year, Clarkia,[47] Calliopsis,[43] Candytuft,[44] Erysimum,[52] Mignonette,[68] Nemophila,[70] Perennial and Sweet Pea,[79] Larkspur.[50]

October 8—Forty-first Week.

Seasonable time for planting in the O. A.,[14] or starting in pots,[21] etc., for forcing, the hardy

bulbs of Hyacinth,[61] Tulip,[79] Crocus,[49] Narcissus,[69] Jonquil,[69] Lilium Longiflorum,[65] Iris,[62] Crown Imperial,[48] Snowdrop,[55] etc.....After sharp frosts, take up, dry and store away for winter, Canna,[44] Caladium,[42] Dahlia,[49] Amaryllis,[37] Gladiolus,[59] Tigridia,[79] and Tuberose,[80] bulbs, etc.....Commence drying off Vallota.[81]

October 15—Forty-second Week.

*Give plants in the Con., W., and the C. P., an abundance of air[21] [24] daily as long as the weather will admit, and also during winter.... By no chance allow a higher temperature[20] [24] to exist at night than would be suitable in the daytime, neither strive to keep as high a degree in cloudy weather as in clear; never subject plants of any kind, and especially Roses, to strong drafts of air ; open ventilators in the Con. on the side away from the wind, in cold weather. ....Secure Lemon Verbena[36] plants....*Haul manure, sand, etc., under shelter for winter use... See "Taking up Plants in the Fall"[15] ....On Insects, Watering, etc.—see Dec. 17.

October 22—Forty-third Week.

Take up Feverfews,[53] Penstemons,[72] Veronicas,[61] for stock plants....Oleanders and other hard wooded plants named under March 26, may be placed in winter quarters....*Water Callas[43] abundantly.*

October 29—Forty-fourth Week.

Sweet Alyssum,[38] Mignonette,[68] Ten-week Stock,[78] Maurandia,[18] Browalia,[41] etc., may be sown for winter and spring decoration.... *Young plants of Carnation, Chrysanthemum, Stevia, Eupatorium, Pink, Violet, that are too small for flowering, may be kept safely during winter at a night temperature of 40° to 45°....*Roses,[25] Deutzias,[50] Dicentras,[51] Lily of the. Valley,[66] Pinks,[14] Daisies,[49] Violets,[61] Astilbe Japonica,[39] for winter and spring forcing, may be taken up, potted, and stored in the C. P. or cellar....*In taking them in from the C. P., etc., during winter, never commence forcing too rapidly ; the same with hardy bulbs.*

November 5—Forty-fifth Week.

*Hardy bulbs named under Oct. 8, may be planted in the O. A. as long as the ground remains open, and be started for forcing two months yet....Fall struck cuttings and seedling plants in small pots should be shifted as required....*Be very particular not to allow the seedlings named under Aug. 20 to become root-bound.

November 12—Forty-sixth Week.

At this season the grounds should be cleaned up generally; vases, etc., secured; rubbish and dead plants removed; manure applied; beds worked over,[12] etc.....*Earliest started bulbs, for forcing, named under Oct. 8, may be brought in. ....Care of Ferneries, see page,[61] and Dec. 24.*

November 19—Forty-seventh Week.

Protect, by laying down or otherwise, Roses,[31] shrubs, etc., before winter sets in severely; mulch the roots for a good distance around....*For airing, temperature, etc., of the*

.

www.ingramcontent.com/pod-product-compliance
Lightning Source LLC
Chambersburg PA
CBHW020306090426
42735CB00009B/1239